Recipes & Ramblings

OLDIE PUBLICATIONS

First published in 2010
by Oldie Publications Ltd
65 Newman Street, London W1T 3EG
www.theoldie.co.uk

ISBN-10: 1-901170-12-8
ISBN-13: 978-1-901170-12-2

A catalogue record for this book
is available from the British Library

Printed and bound in the UK by
Butler, Tanner & Dennis Ltd

Recipes & Ramblings

Written and illustrated by
Elisabeth Luard

From her column in *The* 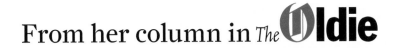Oldie

About the author

ELISABETH LUARD has published more than a dozen cookery books including *European Peasant Cookery*, *The Food of Spain and Portugal*, *European Festival Food* and *The Latin American Kitchen*; plus two novels and three autobiographies with recipes, including *Family Life: Birth, Death and the Whole Damn Thing* (Guild of Food Writer's Award, 1996). She has just completed her first decade as *The Oldie*'s cookery columnist and writes regularly in several national newspapers and magazines, including *Country Living*, where she also provides her own illustrations.

Work as an artist/illustrator predates Elisabeth's work as a food writer, and she uses a sketchbook and watercolours rather than a camera to record images and recipes on her travels. As a bird painter she has had two solo exhibitions at the Tryon Gallery.

Awards include the 2007 Glenfiddich Food Writer of the Year for her columns in *The Oldie*, as well as several Guild of Food Writers' Awards for books and journalism. She lives in a remote farmhouse in Wales and grows her own cabbages in spite of strong competition from the slugs.

Contents

Introduction

The illustrations in this book are from my own working sketchbooks accumulated over the years – I take my culinary and place-notes in watercolour – and the intention is to illuminate rather than instruct. As for the choice of recipes, these, while extracted from the full ten years of articles in *The Oldie*, have been rearranged in conventional cookbook order, sometimes with new or altered introductions, bearing in mind that recipes are all the more usable for knowing how the finished dish should look and taste and where it comes from and why. Cooking is too inexact a science, subject to unknowable interventions – size of eggs, dampness of flour, brawniness of arm – to lend itself to the garage manual approach.

Behind every great chef there's a granny, their own or someone else's. I've never yet met a chef who, one way or another, didn't acknowledge a debt to his female ancestors. The French have a name for it – *cuisine grandmère*. Which is much the same as home cooking, but carries, I'm happy to say – having achieved no less than seven grannyhoods myself – greater authority.

You will find no drizzlings or drapings at grandma's table – perish the thought. In southern

Spain, where my own culinary habits were formed, dishes which fall into the category of granny cooking are slow-simmered stews of the kind my own children called 'beans and bones'. Not so much recipes as reactions, based on the pulses and vegetables which came most easily to hand, enriched with olive oil and flavoured with a bit of ham bone, Spain's universal stock cube, or maybe a joint of an old boiling fowl – honest cooking, family food, nothing grand but good enough for the grandest table when prepared with care. Now my children are adult and flown, such dishes remain the welcome-home food, a reminder of childhood, comforting to the spirit as well as nourishment for the body.

Heroines? Quite a few. Julia Child for one. Anyone checking the obituaries in August 2004 could not have failed to notice the passing of Mrs Child – TV chef, food historian, upholder of female rights and upsetter of corporate America's apple-carts – at the far-from-finished age of ninety-one. A tall, big-boned woman with a frizz of auburn hair, an upper-crust New England drawl and a master's from ultra-posh Smith College, Julia was not an obvious candidate for popular success. More John Wayne than Doris Day, she gutted chickens, skinned rabbits and scooped the poached salmon back on the dish after she'd dropped it on the floor. And if the recipe didn't work, she didn't reshoot it, she fixed it.

Ever since I first came across a copy of Mrs Child's *Mastering the Art of French Cooking* in the English bookshop in Paris, Julia was my lode-star. As with all heroines, I never thought I'd meet her. And then in 1986, just after the US publication of my first book, *European Peasant Cookery*, having been invited to address Boston's Association of Culinary Historians, an unmistakeable figure stumped through the seated audience to take her place in the front row. Meanwhile, the historians had done me the nerve-wracking honour of cooking some of the more substantial recipes from my book as a taster after the talk. Julia, however, had other plans. I might admire and even sample the cassoulet prepared in my name, but then we – Julia and her husband Paul and a few friends – would slip away for a proper meal at Legal Seafood, Boston's most celebrated fish eatery.

What could I do but agree? Everyone ate prodigiously. Except myself. Unfortunately for my reputation as a trencherwoman, it was by then too late to explain that I'd gone through the identical menu two hours earlier with an interviewer from the *Boston Globe*. All I remember of the meal is a bucketful of little-neck clams apiece and a pyramid of grilled lobster between us. But I do remember that my hosts were horrified by what was happening to food production in the US.

'Convenience food is fake food,' said Julia, using a lobster claw for emphasis. 'All it does is fool the gut into thinking it's being fed. And health food is worse. How can anyone eat the stuff? Have a little more melted butter – it really works with the clams.'

There was talk, too, of the Special Relationship. During World War Two Julia's husband Paul had run the war room for the OSS, forerunner of the CIA, an organisation modelled on the British Secret Service which, as I recall from my childhood, operated out of a bunker in Curzon Street alongside the Lansdowne Club – frequented by my grandfather, a senior Royal Air Force man with more than a few friends who wore pulled-down fedoras and belted their trenchcoats. Unofficial access to the bunker appeared to be via a café at the back of the swimming pool where, in

> *'Convenience food is fake food,' said Julia Child, using a lobster claw for emphasis. And health food is worse. How can anyone eat the stuff? Have a little more melted butter – it really works with the clams'*

spite of post-war rationing, they did a fine frankfurter in a crusty white roll spread with real butter.

Mrs Child was always on the side of the angels, kind to the inexperienced and tolerant of other people's mistakes. She refused lucrative product endorsements and took public issue with the purveyors of fast food who were, she felt, largely responsible for the ill health of the American nation. Not bad for a life's work.

Elizabeth David, on the other hand, was in the grand old tradition of literary lions – reclusive, difficult and, at least in old age, rather too fond of the bottle. Her effect on my contemporaries, followers in the footsteps of Constance Spry and inclined to complicated presentations, was as liberating as fresh air after a storm. Her recipes are written conversationally – none of your step-by-step instruction and precious few weights and measures – and deliver the spirit as well as the practical instructions without which a cookbook can't do what it's supposed to do. The late and just-as-great Jane Grigson explained her contemporary's appeal: 'Every time we begin to feel fussed by the cookery elaborators with their flashy tricks and colour photos, we can restore confidence by returning to Elizabeth David.'

> ❝ *I met Elizabeth David once only, in her kitchen supply shop. She inspected me from head to foot and implied that the articles I sought were unlikely to be within my budget* ❞

I met the great woman once only, in her kitchen supply shop just behind Sloane Square in the early 1970s. She was moving baskets around the narrow basement corridor and we had a conversation about my wish to purchase the little heart-shaped white china draining pots required for the preparation of *coeurs à la crème*.

Mrs David inspected me from head to foot – admittedly I might have looked as if I didn't have two brass farthings to rub together, what with the Tibetan boots, the full-length Moroccan *djellaba* and the four small children testing out the hand-carved wooden spoons on the undersides of the copper-

bottomed pots and pans – and implied that the articles I sought were unlikely to be within my budget.

Too bad, bog off, was more or less the message – as indeed it was for rather too many of her customers, since shortly afterwards she left the business which bore her name. Not much of an encounter, you might think. However, when I embarked on my own career as a cookery writer and was preparing an article on influential food writers for a column in the *Field*, my first employer in the genre, I took courage in both hands and enquired of Mrs David's good friend Alan Davidson – co-founder with Mrs D of the Oxford Symposium on Food and Cookery – whether the great woman, given a sympathetic recommendation, might be prepared to grant an interview.

'Not a chance,' said he. 'On the other hand, no need. Read *An Omelette and a Glass of Wine*. It's all there.' Indeed it is. A collection of elegant, sharply observed journalism first published in 1984, Mrs David enjoyed her time at the *Spectator* under Iain Hamilton and hated the editorial shears wielded by Ernestine Carter at the *Sunday Times*. 'What matters,' she wrote in her introduction, 'is sympathetic editors who know how to get the best out of their contributors.'

Quite so. And if the experience of a lifetime can be summed up in a recipe book – as I believe it can – then those of us who write about food are indeed fortunate to find ourselves in the hands of a sympathetic editor. Without Richard Ingrams, not only would there not have been a chance to celebrate ten years of whatever popped into my head, but I – and maybe you too – wouldn't have had half the fun.

Elisabeth Luard, 2010

Chapter 1
Soups & Starters

Every meal has to start somewhere. And the act of setting something quick and easy on the table – a light soup, a plate of smoked fish or wind-dried ham, or a scoopable purée to eat with bread and olives – sets the scene for what's to follow. Any soup served as a starter should be a one-note affair in which a single flavour predominates. Whether the basis is fish or vegetables or chicken or meat, or even milk or wine, the primary flavouring should be easily identifiable – peas or leeks or tomato or asparagus or mushrooms or onions – all of which are classic first-course soups.

Start as you mean to go on. If your main course is what the cooks of these islands do best – the roast with all the trimmings – choose potted shrimps with melba toast, smoked mackerel flaked into soured cream, smoked salmon with brown bread and butter. The same principle can be applied to all other culinary traditions. If your choice today is northern Italian, serve a plate of Parma ham with bread-sticks and unsalted butter as a starter. If Latino is what you fancy, skip the guacamole in favour of perfectly ripe avocados with lime-quarters and salt. If the thrust of the meal is bourgeois French, start with a hot soup in winter, chilled in summer – sorrel or watercress, or an elegant vichyssoise with a curl of cream and sprinkle of chives. If you're heading for Greece or Turkey, set out a pretty plateful of olives, peppers cooked in oil, sliced tomatoes dressed with finely chopped garlic and parsley.

If you're contemplating something Spanish – maybe a paella with rabbit and snails, as they like it in Valencia, or with crayfish and wild asparagus, as they like it in Andalusia, where my four children went to school – get into the mood with a long iced glassful of garlicky gazpacho and a plate of sliced chorizo.

In short, keep it simple.

Fresh pea soup

Make this delicate soup in early summer with the first of the tender young homegrown peas. Buy them in the pod while still bright green and sappy.

Serves 4–6

POD THE PEAS, saving both peas and pods.

Bring the pods to the boil in 2 pints of water, a few peppercorns, a little salt and the onion trimmings. Turn down the heat, lid loosely and simmer for 30 minutes, till the pods are mushy. Strain out the solids and return the stock to the pan (you'll need 1 ½ pints of liquid). Add the peas, diced potato and spring onion and bring all to the boil. Turn down and simmer for about 20 minutes, till the potato is perfectly tender. Drop everything in the liquidiser and process to a purée. Taste, season, return to the pan, and reheat. Whisk in the butter just before serving. You can, if you must, finish each bowlful with a swirl of cream and a sprig of mint.

Ingredients
- 2 lbs peas in pod
- 2–3 spring onions, trimmed and chopped (save the trimmings)
- 1 medium potato, peeled and diced
- Salt and pepper
- 1 tablespoon unsalted butter

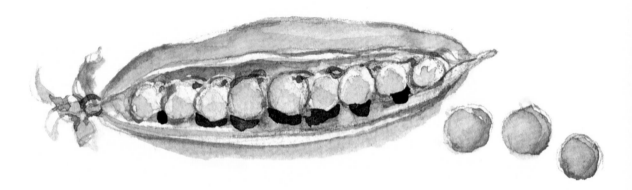

Soupe bonne femme

Anything described as *cuisine de bonne femme*, 'housewife's cooking', tells you the recipe is variable and seasonal – *soupe bonne femme* is a generic term for any soup you can whip up in a minute with whatever's popped up in the *jardin potager*. This version is a winter warmer from northern France, dairy country, and can be finished with a swirl of cream rather than butter. Purists would use only the white part of the leek: feel free to please yourself.

Serves 4–6

PUT THE CHOPPED leeks and half the butter in a heavy pan and cook over a very gentle heat for 10–15 minutes. Don't let the leeks brown.

Meanwhile, in another pan, bring the consommé or broth to boiling point. Add the potatoes and the boiling broth to the leeks. Taste and add salt if necessary, bring back to the boil, turn down the heat and simmer gently till the potatoes are cooked and the leeks dispersed throughout. Bring the milk to the boil and stir it in. Liquidise to a purée, or mash and leave the texture rough. Whisk in the rest of the butter just before serving.

Ingredients
- 4 medium-sized leeks, white part only, finely chopped
- About 3 oz butter
- 1 pint clear consommé or strong chicken broth
- 3 peeled and quartered potatoes, thinly sliced
- 1 pint full-cream milk
- Salt

Sorrel soup

Butter, egg yolks and cream enrich a plain chicken broth sharpened with sorrel, one of several combinations known to the housewives of France as *soupe bonne femme* (see page 19). This is the version recommended by E S Dallas, Victorian culinary expert and author of *Kettner's Book of the Table*, who describes the dish as 'a culinary portrait uniting two principal concepts of womanhood as symbolised in the malleability of cream and the acidity of sorrel.' Fancy that.

Serves 4–6

MELT MOST OF the butter in a pan, add the sorrel and a little salt, and sauté for a few minutes on a low flame. Pour on the boiling chicken broth and simmer for 30 minutes. Stir the egg yolks together and, taking the saucepan off the fire, pour a little broth onto the yolks, stirring quickly, before returning the mixture to the pan. Continue to stir the soup over a gentle heat, so that the liaison of eggs and broth is successfully brought about and a homogeneously smooth consistency is achieved. Pour in the cream, stir in what is left of the butter, and serve this suave soup with French bread which has been five minutes in a hot oven, or with melba toast (split any leftover breakfast toast and dry it in the oven).

Ingredients
- 4 oz butter
- 4–5 generous handfuls sorrel, shredded into fine ribbons
- 2 pints chicken broth, heated to boiling point
- 2 small egg yolks (or yolk from 1 large egg)
- 4–5 tablespoons double cream
- A little salt

Nettle soup

Choose a nice clean patch of nettles, snip off the top four leaves only, and don't forget to wear gloves. The sting, you'll be happy to know, disappears when heat is applied. Watercress and spinach make an acceptable substitute for the nettle-tops, should your botanical courage fail you.

Serves 4–6

RINSE THE NETTLES and shake them dry. Leave half of them whole and shred the other half (use gloves). Reserve.

Cook the onions gently in a nugget of butter until they soften. Add the whole nettle leaves and turn them to blend. Add the diced potatoes and 1 ½ pints water. Bring to the boil, turn down to simmer, lid loosely and cook for 20 minutes, until the potato is perfectly soft.

Process the soup to a purée. Season and return it to the heat with the shredded leaves. Let it bubble for a moment or two. Off the heat, stir in the cream.

Ingredients
- About 1 pint nettle-tops (about 8 oz)
- 4 shallots or 12 spring onions, finely chopped
- Large knob butter
- 2 large potatoes, peeled and diced
- ½ pint double cream
- Salt and pepper

Mexican chicken soup

A bowlful of chicken broth, *caldo*, fortified with *chilaquiles*, finely sliced tortillas crisped in a little hot oil, is served as a do-it-yourself assembly which varies according to what's at hand. The only essential is a seasoning of chilli, nature's stomach disinfectant. Mexican mothers consider a baby of six months not too young for a little taste of chilli on the tongue to build up tolerance – essential in a steamy climate where fridges remain a luxury.

Serves 4–6

BRING THE BROTH to the boil. Add the chicken breast and simmer for about 10 minutes till the meat is perfectly firm. Remove the chicken with a draining spoon, then shred. Meanwhile heat a finger's width of oil in a frying pan and fry the tortilla strips, a few at a time, till puffed and crisp. Transfer to kitchen paper to drain. Reheat the broth to boiling point.

Provide bowls and spoons and set everything out on the table for everyone to fill their bowl with the combination of their choice.

Finish with a ladleful of the boiling broth, a sprinkle of diced chilli and a squeeze of lime.

Ingredients

- 1 ½ pints chicken broth
- 1–2 skinned, boneless chicken breasts
- oil for shallow frying
- 4–6 cornmeal tortillas, sliced into narrow strips
- lime quarters
- 1 green chilli, de-seeded and diced

Additions (choose 2–3)

- 1–2 large ripe tomatoes, skinned, de-seeded and diced
- 2–3 spring onions, finely chopped
- 1 ripe avocado, stoned, skinned and diced
- A few sprigs fresh coriander and/or mint leaves, roughly chopped
- About 4 oz grated cheddar-type cheese

Rillettes de porc

Potted pork, smooth-textured and generously spiced, makes a simple hors d'oeuvre to serve with radishes, cornichons and chunks of crisp baguette. Commercially prepared lard won't do. To prepare your own pork lard you need *panne de porc*, the soft white fat which surrounds the kidney.

Have a bowl of hot water ready to rinse your fingers to prevent sticking, and then strip the little white fat globules from the membrane. Melt the fat very slowly in a heavy pan or low oven with enough water to prevent browning. Save any crisp little scraps to top a salad instead of croutons.

Makes about 2 lbs

MELT THE PORK LARD (or goose fat) gently in a heavy pan – don't let it bubble – add the chunked pork and stir over a very low heat till the fat runs. Add a tablespoon of water, salt, pepper and all-spice, tuck in the bouquet garni, and leave to cook very gently for 3 hours or more, or bake in the lowest possible oven – 75C/165F – till the fat is completely melted and the meat absolutely soft.

Keep a careful watch for sticking, stirring the pieces regularly with a wooden spoon. The fat should never bubble and the temperature should stay very low throughout the cooking. At the end, there should be no more water and the fat should be clear and the meat meltingly soft.

Remove the bouquet garni and skim off a ladleful of the surface-fat. Using two forks, pull the meat into fine shreds. Taste and adjust the seasoning.

Pot up in small jars or empty yoghurt pots, and leave to cool. Seal under a layer of the reserved fat and refrigerate till firm. Ready immediately, though it'll keep for a month in the fridge as long as the surface is not disturbed. The same method can be applied to goose or duck.

Serve with baguette or freshly toasted sourdough.

Ingredients
- 6 oz freshly made pork lard (or, alternatively, goose fat)
- 3 lbs skinned pork belly, chunked
- 3 teaspoons salt
- 1 teaspoon freshly milled pepper
- 1 teaspoon powdered allspice
- Bouquet garni (thyme, rosemary, bay)

Omelette fines herbes

Simple, delicious and so easy to get right or wrong, says Geraldene Holt in *Diary of a French Herb Garden* (Pavilion, 2003). Choose a well-tempered omelette pan about 18 cm in diameter.

To temper a raw-iron pan, heat a couple of tablespoons of oil in the pan till it smokes, add a tablespoon of rough-grain salt and rub with a ball of newspaper till the oil has been absorbed.

Serves 1 hungry gardener or 2 more modest appetites

FORK THE EGGS lightly together with a drop of cold water, salt and freshly ground pepper. Chop the herbs finely and stir them into the eggs – don't over-beat.

Have ready a warm plate.

Heat the omelette pan and drop in the nugget of butter. Wait till it froths and roll it round the pan. Pour in the egg mixture and roll it around. The bottom will set immediately. Pull the edges to the middle to allow the uncooked egg to feel the heat. As soon as the top begins to set, drop in the last nugget of butter, flip a third of the omelette over to enclose the middle and roll it out onto the warm plate to make a bolster shape. That's all.

Ingredients
- 3 free-range eggs
- Small handful flat-leaf parsley, chives, tarragon, chervil
- Sea salt, pepper
- 1 walnut-sized nugget unsalted butter

To finish
- Another nugget unsalted butter

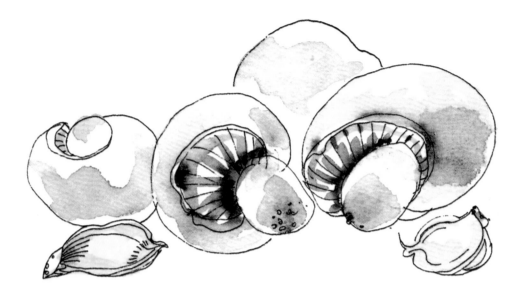

Mushrooms à la grecque

AN EASY LITTLE Greek mezze – a godsend to the cook-hostess struggling to keep up standards in the Sixties – as recommended by Patience Gray in *The Centaur's Kitchen* (Prospect, 2008), a happily discursive instruction manual for Chinese and Lascar cooks aboard *SS Centaur*, a passenger ship of the Blue Funnel Line working the ports of the Mediterranean through the middle of the last century. I have listed the ingredients for ease of use, but left the method in the writer's own words.

Serves 8 (the number of passengers at table on the ship)

'**THE CLASSICAL WAY** with cauliflower florets, celery hearts, young artichoke hearts, root fennel (*finocchio*), tender white mushrooms, small pickling onions, leeks, is to prepare an aromatic court-bouillon consisting of three parts water to one part olive oil, with lemon juice, salt, coriander seeds, peppercorns and a bouquet garni of parsley, thyme, fennel, celery, bay leaf.

'The liquor is boiled for five minutes, the selected vegetables are thrown in and cooked rapidly till tender. The vegetable is then strained, set on a dish and served with a little of the reduced cooking liquor, garnished with chopped parsley, cold as an hors d'oeuvre.'

Ingredients
- 2 lbs perfectly fresh button mushrooms, wiped and finely sliced
- ¾ pint water
- ¼ pint olive oil
- 2 tablespoons lemon juice
- 1 teaspoon coriander seeds
- Bouquet garni (bay, thyme, parsley)
- Salt

To finish
- Parsley

Chopped liver

Here's what Jay Rayner's mum – aka Agony Auntie Claire – prepares for the cold supper served on the Jewish Sabbath.

Serves 4–6

FRY THE ONION gently in the fat till soft and golden. Remove and reserve.

Rinse the chicken livers very thoroughly and sprinkle them with salt. Reheat the pan and roast the chicken livers in the dry pan till they change colour, turning them once.

Chop the liver and onion together to make a coarse-textured paté. Combine the mixture with the chopped egg (save a spoonful for decoration). Taste and season, pile on a dish and finish with the remaining chopped egg.

Serve with matzo, salt-pickled cucumbers and pickled herring.

Ingredients

- 1 medium onion, finely chopped
- 2–3 tablespoons chicken or goose fat
- 12 oz chicken livers, trimmed
- 2 hard-boiled eggs, shelled and finely chopped
- Salt and freshly ground pepper

Patience Gray's chicken liver paté

You'll find the ready-made version of this classic paté in every *traiteur* from Paris to Marseilles, sold by weight and eaten in combination with other prepared dishes from the same source – French housewives take pride in patronising the best *traiteur* in town. You'll find more of the same in Patience Gray's *Plats du Jour* (reprinted by Persephone books, 2006), a compendium of the classic dishes of the French bourgeoisie from one of the original translators of *Larousse Gastronomique*. I have listed the ingredients for convenience of use, but left unaltered Ms Gray's account of the method.

Serves 4–5

'A POUND OF chicken livers will make sufficient paté for four or five people. For each pound of chicken livers you need 4 oz butter; 1 small glass of brandy; 1 small glass of sherry; black pepper; salt; a pinch of allspice and a pinch of powdered herbs (thyme, marjoram, basil). Melt 2 oz butter in a pan and very gently sauté the chicken livers for barely 3 minutes.

'They should still be pink inside. Remove them, and add the glass of sherry and the glass of cognac to the juices in the pan. Cook for a few moments. Mash the livers to a fine paste with salt, pepper, spice and herbs, the squeezed juice of a garlic clove and the remaining butter. Add the liquor from the pan and put this composition into a small earthenware terrine. Chill.

'Serve with melba toast. Note: It is perfectly possible to use deep-frozen chicken livers provided they are given the opportunity to de-freeze. This can take as long as 5–6 hours at room temperature. If they are de-frozen by artificial means they lose all taste and are tough.'

Ingredients
- 1 lb chicken livers
- 4 oz butter
- 1 small glass brandy
- 1 small glass sherry
- Powdered herbs (thyme, marjoram, basil)
- 1 garlic clove
- Allspice, black pepper, salt

Egyptian bessara

This garlicky bean purée is traditionally made with dried fava beans (you can buy them ready-skinned). You can substitute any of the other pulse vegetables which provide vegetarians with much of their protein – haricots, butterbeans, chickpeas, lentils.

Serves 4–6

TIP EVERYTHING in the food processor and whizz till smooth. Tip into a bowl and finish, if you like, with a handful of torn coriander leaves, pitted green olives, finely chopped spring onions or a small green chilli, de-seeded and finely chopped. Serve with one of the Middle Eastern scooping breads – *pitta*, *pide* or Lebanese *khoubiz* – warmed in the oven.

Ingredients

- 1 lb ready-cooked skinned fava beans, drained
- 2–3 garlic cloves, skinned and roughly chopped
- 2 tablespoons white wine vinegar
- 4 tablespoons olive oil
- 1 teaspoon ground cumin
- ½ teaspoon chilli powder
- 2 tablespoons freshly chopped mint
- Salt and pepper

To finish

- 2 tablespoons chopped, pitted green olives
- 2 tablespoons chopped coriander leaves
- 1 small green chilli, de-seeded and finely chopped
- 2–3 spring onions, finely chopped

Potted grouse

An all-purpose recipe which works with any elderly game bird, from *bon viveur* and grouse-fancier Clarissa Dickson Wright. Any tough old fowl is suitable for potting in similar fashion: pheasant, partridge, rook, pigeon, duck, guinea fowl, goose, even an old boiling hen past her laying-days.

Serves 6–8

PREHEAT THE oven to 170C/325F/Gas3. Cut the birds in half and rub the fleshy sides with the seasoning.

Put the giblets in a heavy casserole and lay the birds on top. Add the stock, cover and cook in the oven for 2 hours, or until the flesh falls from the bones. When it's cool enough to handle, remove the meat, discarding the bones, and shred into small pieces by hand. Mix the softened butter with the meat and port and enough of the cooking liquor to moisten. Press into a large pot, or several small ones. Chill. Cover with melted clarified butter and leave to set.

Bring up to room temperature before serving. Lasts up to 3 weeks in the fridge, much longer in the freezer.

Ingredients
- 4 elderly grouse with their giblets (or 4 partridges or 2 pheasants)
- 1 tablespoon seasoning (mixed salt, pepper, cayenne)
- ½ pint game or chicken stock
- 6 oz softened butter
- 4 oz melted clarified butter
- 1 tablespoon port

Chapter 2
Fish

If wild fish are pricey, sustainability an issue, and fish farms the cause of many an ecological mess-up, go for the cheapest on the slab. The cheaper the fish, the fresher and more locally caught it's likely to be. Bargains you can safely consume without a twinge of conscience are the dark-fleshed beauties: mackerel and members of the herring family, including pilchards and their closest relative, the Mediterranean sardine, recorded in 2009 for the first time in Cornish waters – a timely indication that the seas are warming up.

> *As a nation, we've never had much of a taste for fresh fish, though flatfish find a ready market, as do prawns, scallops and mussels. For the rest, our traditional taste is for preserved, salt-cured fish*

Tuna and swordfish are sufficiently endangered to omit from the menu altogether for as long as it takes to restore the breeding stock. Crustaceans, the vultures of the sea – dustbin-men whose responsibility is to clean up everyone else's leavings, our own included – are plentiful round our shores, and lobsters, a particular high-value inshore harvest, are regularly replenished in the wild with tank-reared juveniles. Mussels are an equally convenient crop, needing nothing more to settle down and thrive than a convenient post or rope set in sheltered waters with access to a wild food source. Open them in a splash of wine (or a ladleful of seawater), bubble them up with cream, shower them with parsley, then ladle them into bowls.

Salmon farmers, under pressure from ecologists and informed customers looking for quality, have smartened up their act of recent years, and the best farmed salmon is by no means inferior to fish from the wild. In Mrs Beeton's day, when farmed fish was not an option, a well-grown salmon – a forty-pounder was by no means unusual – was an economical purchase, appearing in different guises at successive meals in much the same way as the Sunday joint.

As for the rest of our diminishing stocks of sea fish, most of what remains is shipped to Continental markets where people are prepared to pay the price to keep the fishermen in business. Which, were it not for the popularity of fish and chips and our increased awareness of what other people like to eat, would not be considered much of a loss. As a nation, we've never had much of a taste for fresh fish, though flatfish find a ready market, as do prawns, scallops and mussels. For the rest, our traditional taste is for preserved, salt-cured fish – herring, cod, haddock, salmon, trout, mackerel, sprats, eel – smoked to increase shelf-life, an additional precaution in a damp climate.

Salt-cod salad with red pepper dressing

A combination of salt-cod and sweet peppers, known in Catalonia, its land of origin, as *xató* (pronounced 'chat-oh'), of which the most important element is the dressing, *salsa romesco*. Somewhere between a sauce and a dip, and a speciality of Tarragona, a *romesco* is the automatic accompaniment to *escalivets*, green onions chargrilled and eaten like asparagus. The precise composition of the salsa is a matter for vigorous argument. Some wouldn't dream of including peppers at all, confining themselves to garlic and almonds. Others avoid any mention of lettuce and stick to tomatoes and onions. Best not discuss it with the natives but go your own sweet way. Anything salty, chewy and flakeable will do for the fish element if you don't have salt-cod – kipper fillets, smoked mackerel, smoked salmon.

Serves 4–6

GRILL OR BARBECUE or roast the tomatoes, peppers and garlic cloves on a high heat till soft and lightly caramelised – don't let them burn. Skin and de-seed as appropriate.

Meanwhile, brown the nuts and breadcrumbs in a little hot oil and pound to a paste with a pestle and mortar, or whizz up in the food processor. Work in the roasted vegetable pulp and beat well. Add the olive oil in a thin stream, as if making mayonnaise, working in a little vinegar from time to time, till you have a thick spoonable purée: you're looking for a soft mayonnaise-like emulsion which holds its shape on the spoon. If the mixture splits, work a corner with a little boiling water until the emulsion reforms. Taste and season with salt and chilli. Toss the salsa with the salad ingredients, or serve each element separately for people to choose their own combinations.

The sauce also makes a particularly fine dip for raw or grilled vegetables or seafood – prawns, lobster, shrimp, brochettes from the barbecue. Make it in quantity and keep it in the fridge instead of that dismal pink stuff sold in jars as seafood sauce.

Ingredients

Salsa romesco
- 1 lb firm, ripe tomatoes
- 2 red peppers
- 1 whole garlic head, broken into cloves
- 4 oz hazelnuts or almonds (or a mixture of both)
- 4 tablespoons fresh breadcrumbs
- About ¼ pint olive oil
- 2 tablespoons red wine vinegar
- 1 teaspoon sea salt
- ½ teaspoon ground chilli

The salad
- 1 curly endive (also known as chicory or *frisée*)
- 2 oz dried tuna fish (*tonyina*) or 1 small tin tuna in oil, flaked
- 2 oz pre-soaked salt-cod or other fish, shredded
- Small tin anchovies in oil, drained
- A handful of olives (green or black)

KLIPFISKE/SALTFISK

Frugal Portuguese salt-cod bake

While salt-cod is no longer poor folks' food, and most of the Mediterranean's supplies come from Norway's Lofoten Islands rather than Portugal (Henningsvær, above, is the Lofoten region's most active fishing village), Catholic Europe still has a taste for what was considered a properly abstemious dish for Fridays and the eve of every saint's day. Anyone who's forgotten how to penny-pinch and still eat well need look no further than Fiona Beckett's *The Frugal Cook* (Absolute Press, 2009). Smoked haddock is an acceptable substitute for the cod.

Serves 6–8

PUT THE COD in a roomy pan with enough fresh cold water to cover, bring slowly to the boil and simmer over a low heat for 7–8 minutes, till tender. Drain, reserving a little of the cooking water. Remove skin and bones, flake and set aside.

Heat the olive oil with half the butter, add the onions and fry gently till soft. Add the garlic, stir in the flour, then gradually add the milk and bubble up till thickened. Add the bay leaf and capers and leave to infuse over a low heat. Stir in the flaked fish and thin the sauce with a little of the reserved cooking water.

Meanwhile, bring the sliced potatoes to the boil from cold water, then drain them. Oil a gratin dish, spread a third of the potatoes on the base, cover with half the eggs and half the fish and onions. Repeat the layers, finishing with potato. Brush the tops of the potatoes with the remaining butter, melted. Bake at 190C/375F/Gas5 for 45–50 minutes, till the filling is bubbling and the potatoes nicely browned. Serve with a sharply dressed green salad, says Ms Beckett.

Ingredients
- 1 ½ lbs ready-soaked salt-cod
- 4 tablespoons olive oil
- 2 oz butter
- 2–3 large mild onions, thinly sliced
- 2 large garlic cloves, chopped
- 1 tablespoon flour
- 1 pint whole milk
- 1 bay leaf
- 1 heaped tablespoon small capers
- 2 teaspoons wine vinegar
- About 2 lbs potatoes, scrubbed and thinly sliced
- 3–4 hard-boiled eggs, peeled and cut into wedges
- Salt and freshly ground pepper

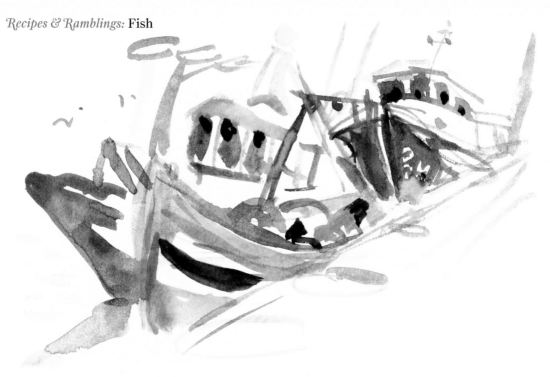

Baked sea-bass with dill and caviar cream

The time a fish takes to cook depends on its thickness: this may sound obvious, but one can forget that a middle cut of a large fish will take much longer to cook than a whole smaller fish.

Sustainability is always an issue with seafood. The jury's still out (and likely to remain so) on the consequences of farming the sea, though certain fish are more suitable than others. Sea-bass, a ferocious predator in the wild, though lacking the salmon's urge to roam, adapts well to captive conditions in the fish-pens at the eastern end of the Mediterranean, making it one of the cheapest and most widely available of all our farmed fish.

Serves 4–6

PREHEAT THE OVEN to 220C/425F/Gas7.

Let the fish come up to room temperature and wipe it thoroughly, removing any blood clots in the cavity. Oil it inside and out, season with salt and pepper, and stuff the cavity with the lemon. Wrap neatly in foil, shiny side inwards, folding it over the top with a pleat to make sure the juices don't escape. Bake for 20 minutes without opening the oven. Remove, but don't open the packet. Let the fish cool in its foil for an hour. By then it will still be warm and juicy, but perfectly cooked. Meanwhile, make the sauce: combine the soured cream with the dill and the caviar. That's all.

Ingredients
- 1 large farmed sea-bass (about 4lbs), gutted and scaled
- Olive oil
- 1 lemon, roughly chopped
- Sea salt and roughly ground pepper

The sauce
- ½ pint soured cream
- Small jar Danish caviar
- Small bunch dill, finely chopped

Whole poached salmon

To poach a whole fish, you need a fish kettle of the appropriate size. If this is not available, curl it into a large roasting tin and lid tightly with foil.

A 12-lb salmon serves 20

PUT THE FISH in the kettle and add enough water to cover it completely. Add sea salt. Bring to the boil. The larger the fish, the longer this takes. Allow it to bubble for 1 minute, then remove from the heat. Leave it to cool. Once cooled – overnight is fine – the fish will be perfectly cooked, tender and juicy.

Serve with a home-made mayonnaise sharpened with the juice of a bitter orange, rather than vinegar or lemon. If you use ready-made mayonnaise, blend it fifty-fifty with Greek strained yoghurt and stir in a tablespoonful of finely grated orange zest. Good with new potatoes dressed with dill.

Ingredients
- 1 large salmon
- Sea salt

Tea-smoked salmon

This is an Oriental way with the king of fish, though the method works just as well with any meaty fish of respectable size.

Serves 6–8

WIPE THE FISH inside and out. Remove the dark red vein which runs down the bone inside the cavity. Sprinkle with the salt, inside and out. Leave in a cool place for a couple of hours. Let it come back to room temperature and dust off excess salt.

Have ready a fish kettle or a large roasting tin with a rack – the fish needs to sit well clear of the smoke. Line the container with foil, shiny side up. Sprinkle in a layer of rice and tea about ¼-inch

thick. Place the fish on the rack. Lid tightly or cover securely with a double layer of foil.

Place the container over a high heat – you'll probably need two burners – and wait until you can smell the smoke. Turn the burners down to medium, open the window and leave the kitchen. Allow 15 minutes for smoke to build up and penetrate the fish. Remove the container from the heat (don't open) and set aside – outside, if you have access.

The fish will continue to cook as it cools. Your reward for a smoke-wreathed kitchen will be moist, succulent fish with an exquisitely delicate flavour. Serve at room temperature.

Plain white rice, and a salad of shredded white radishes and carrots dressed with rice-wine vinegar and toasted sesame oil, would be appropriate accompaniments, though a lemony hollandaise and baby new potatoes would not go amiss.

Ingredients
- A whole small salmon (4–5 lbs cleaned weight), gutted and scaled
- 4–5 teaspoons sea salt
- 2–3 tablespoons uncooked rice
- 2–3 tablespoons China tea leaves (lapsang souchong is perfect)

Koluu's sautéed prawns with spices

Sri Lanka's most famous restauranteur, Hemalallindre Ranawake – better known as Koluu – stir-fries prawns with nuts and lemongrass. All you need is a wok and a camping stove. Just the thing for a steamy evening under the stars.

Serves 4

BEHEAD, PEEL and de-vein the prawns, leaving the tails in place.

Heat 2 tablespoons of the oil in a wok or frying pan over moderate heat and toss the prawns in the hot oil for about 1 ½ minutes. Remove and reserve.

Meanwhile, chop the lemongrass and drop it in the processor along with the onions, garlic, ginger, coconut and almonds or cashews, and grind to a paste – you may need a little water.

Reheat the wok with the remaining oil. Add the curry leaves or bay, stir in the onion paste, turmeric, ground coriander, chilli sauce and salt, and cook gently for 10 minutes to soften the onion. Add the cream and the sugar and bubble up, stirring till smooth. Return the prawns to the pan and cook for another minute.

Transfer to a serving dish and finish with fresh coriander leaves, roughly chopped. Serve with plain-cooked white rice.

Ingredients
- 8–12 large prawns
- 3 tablespoons vegetable oil
- 1 stalk lemongrass, stripped down to the tender core
- 4 medium-sized onions, roughly chopped
- 4–5 garlic cloves, skinned
- 1 thick slice fresh ginger
- 1 tablespoon desiccated coconut
- 2 tablespoons almonds or cashews
- A sprig of curry leaves or 2 bay leaves
- 3 tablespoons ground coriander
- 2 teaspoons ground turmeric
- 1 teaspoon Chinese sweet chilli sauce
- ¼ teaspoon salt
- ¾ pint single cream
- 3 teaspoons brown sugar

To finish
- Coriander leaves

Singaporean laksa lemak

Soupy noodles, a dish rarely found in restaurants, are the Malay equivalent of cottage pie.
As with all such dishes, ingredients are chosen to suit the cook. You can replace the tiger prawns
with diced chicken, filleted fish, squid, mushrooms, roast pork, even hard-boiled eggs.

Serves 4–6

SOAK THE NOODLES for 10 minutes in a bowl in enough boiling water to cover everything generously. De-vein the prawns, salt lightly and leave aside to firm the flesh.

Pound the onion, chilli, nuts and sliced lemongrass (or lemon zest) with the shrimp paste and a little water to moisten (use a food processor or liquidiser). Heat the oil in a heavy saucepan and fry the mixture until the onion is lightly browned and deliciously fragrant. Stir in the curry powder and add the stock. Bring to the boil, turn down the heat and simmer for 20 minutes or so to marry the flavours. Fork up the noodles to separate the strands, drain and add to the soup. Reheat and add the prawns and the bean sprouts. Reheat again, loosely lidded, just long enough for the prawns to turn opaque. Stir in the coconut milk and reheat gently – don't let it boil.

Ladle into individual bowls and finish with torn mint leaves. Serve with lemon or lime quarters and *sambal oelek*.

Ingredients

- 8–10 oz rice vermicelli (glass-noodles or rice sticks)
- About a dozen raw tiger prawns, peeled, tails left on
- 2 smallish onions or 1 large onion, slivered
- 1–2 fresh red chillies, de-seeded and chopped
- 6 candlenuts or brazil or macademia nuts (walnuts, at a pinch)
- 1 stem lemongrass (white only, finely sliced) or zest ½ lemon
- 2 teaspoons shrimp paste (*belachan*) or anchovy sauce (or a couple of tinned anchovies, pounded – let's not be picky)
- 1 tablespoon peanut or sesame oil
- 2 teaspoons curry powder or paste (choose one specially for fish)
- 1 pint chicken or fish stock
- A handful bean sprouts or young green beans, picked over and rinsed
- ½ pint coconut milk or diluted coconut cream
- Salt

To serve

- A few fresh mint leaves (or coriander or parsley)
- Quartered lime or lemon
- *Sambal oelek* (dried chillis soaked and pounded with a little oil and salt)

Chapter 3
Meat

The worrying thing is how little we know about what we eat, particularly our meat products. Even our farmers are bewildered by what goes into the stuff they're obliged to feed their animals reared for meat. Take pigs, for instance. The natural diet of your average porker – omnivorous and opportunist – is essentially the same as ours. The really worrying thing is that a beast with a fine enough palate to appreciate a truffle can't tell the difference between noxious slops and wholesome swill. If I were the Empress of Blandings, I like to think I wouldn't touch the beastly stuff with a disinfected cattle-prod. But then again, I too eat at fast-food joints when the need arises, and my taste buds fail to complain. Fast food says the right thing to the palate, which accounts for its unnatural success.

My neighbours down the road in the Welsh valley I call home – they shall, for fear of unwanted visitations, be nameless – keep a pig. Several, actually. They get their pigs in the spring as little curly-tailed piglets and fatten 'em up through the summer on the peelings and scrapings from their own and other participatory households – foodstuffs, that is, which might otherwise go to waste.

The arrangement has the additional merit of providing a safe and sanitary method of recycling perishable items without recourse to land-fill sites overcrowded with the unwanted carcasses of the nation's stock of ruminants. Every Sunday, the pigs get taken out of the stye for a walk. Every autumn, the pigs get slaughtered. The lean is popped in the freezer (we may be backwoods but we're not backward) and the fat is salted down for bacon or used to add richness to sausages and pies.

If climate and geography dictate the way we like to eat – lush meadows for cattle, grassy uplands for sheep, woodland and moorland for game – our islands are perfectly suited to the rearing of meat animals. Our national eating habits changed a couple of centuries ago, as the population drifted from countryside to town. Mrs Beeton, instructing Victorian households in the proper way to do things, gave detailed instructions for what to do with the leftovers from the Sunday roast – leg or shoulder or crown of lamb, beef on the bone – but did not neglect the secondary cuts as the basis of economical dishes for every day. Our great-grandparents cooked nose-to-tail – a habit of mind in the days when every rural household reared its own animals for slaughter, but of increasingly little relevance when the meat on the butcher's slab comes pre-packed and ready-prepared.

There are signs of a return to an attitude which isn't afraid of unprocessed foodstuffs: writers such as Michael Pollan and Hugh Fearnley-Whittingstall, restaurateurs led by Fergus Henderson and Jamie Oliver may make sense of the whole thing yet.

Scotch eggs

Portable, weatherproof and undeniably a good thing for a picnic on a soft day in the Hebrides – the sketch below was drawn while picnicking on the island of Scalpay. You can make smaller versions with quails' eggs. Good with rhubarb chutney (see page 175).

Serves 3–4

SHELL THE EGGS. Work the meat with the bread-crumbs, forked egg, herb and seasonings to make a firm paste. Have ready a bowl of warm water for rinsing your hands. Divide the sausage mixture into 6 pieces, roll each into a ball, flatten it with your hand and work it up the sides of an egg – easiest if your hands are damp – till it's completely enclosed. Continue till all the eggs are provided with jackets.

Dust each egg through the seasoned flour, roll in the egg-and-milk and then in the breadcrumbs.

Fry on a medium heat in at least 2-fingers' depth of oil till the coating is crisp and brown and the sausage meat completely cooked – it'll feel firm rather than squidgy, and unless you're using a deep-fryer you'll have to turn the eggs to fry the other side.

Ingredients
- 6 small hard-boiled eggs
- 1 lb all-pork sausage meat or twice-ground shoulder pork
- 4 tablespoons fresh breadcrumbs
- 1 egg, forked to blend
- 1 teaspoon dried thyme
- 1 teaspoon ground allspice (optional)
- Salt and freshly ground pepper

To finish
- 1 egg whisked with its own volume of milk
- Seasoned flour for dusting
- Dried breadcrumbs for coating
- Oil for frying

SCALPAY

Honey-roast spareribs

A recipe from tropical Singapore, where I sketched this lush scene. Singapore is the melting-pot of south-east Asia, where Malay cooking skills combine Chinese gastronomic sophistication with the robust flavours of India. Pork is permitted among the Nyonya community, the result of intermarriage between Malay women and immigrant Chinese workers, since Malay Muslim dietary rules didn't apply to Chinese husbands.

Serves 4–6

IF YOUR BUTCHER has not already done so, separate the ribs with a sharp knife. Mix all the remaining ingredients to a paste and rub it in. Arrange the ribs in a single layer in a roasting tin. If you have the time, leave for an hour or two to marinate.

Preheat the oven to 180C/350F/Gas6.

Roast the ribs for 30 minutes. Turn them over and pour in a teacupful of hot water. Roast for another 30 minutes, basting occasionally. Serve with plain white rice, a sambal of diced mango or peach dressed with chopped chilli and a little vinegar, and Chinese plum sauce for dipping. You can make a fair approximation of the latter by blending plum jam with a little vinegar and a good pinch of five-spice powder. Eat with your fingers. You'll need lettuce leaves to wipe off the juice.

Ingredients
- 2 lbs pork spare riblets – meat and bone only
- 3 garlic cloves, crushed with a little salt
- 1 teaspoon five-spice powder (ground star anise, fennel seeds, cinnamon, cloves, szechuan or chilli pepper)
- ½ teaspoon ground black pepper
- 1 tablespoon honey
- 1 tablespoon sesame or sunflower oil
- 3 tablespoons light soy sauce

Melton Mowbray pie

The Melton Mowbray, a round pie with a firm jelly which fits comfortably into the pocket, was the huntsman's traditional midday break when in pursuit of the fox (the illustration below is of horsemen in Lincolnshire as they were preparing to leave for the hunt). In these censorious times, the Melton Mowbray Pie Association has managed to get the recipe designated of Protected Geographical Indication (PGI) by the European Commission, which means that no one but the Association is allowed to call it what it is. In the spirit of rebellion, here's Mr Fred Wright's mother's recipe as supplied to Flo White's English Folk Cookery Association in 1927. Make it at your peril.

Makes a 3-lb pie

SIFT THE FLOUR with the salt. Bring the water to the boil in a large pan with the lard, and boil until the fat melts. Beat in the flour and cook over a low heat until the paste comes away from the sides of the pan. This is a hot-water pastry, and at this point it will look slightly transparent. Tip it out onto a well-floured board, and as soon as it is cool enough to handle, knead it thoroughly, until it is alabaster-smooth. Put the pastry in a plastic bag and leave it to prove in a warm place for 30 minutes.

Cut off a quarter of the pastry and reserve it for the lid (keep it warm). Work the larger piece of pastry into a ball and drop it into a warmed 6-inch diameter cake tin. Press it into the tin till the sides and base are covered and the edge rises about an inch above the edge. Even more skilful is to do this outside the tin (flour the tin first) – it'll drop off the base when it's cool and firm to give you a free-standing pastry case. The temperature is important: if the pastry is too cool, it'll break and crumble when raised; if it is too soft (either too warm or too much fat in the mix) it will fall down the sides of the mould.

Chop the meat and its fat thoroughly by hand, season with salt, pepper and the anchovy essence

Ingredients

The crust
- 1 ¾ lbs strong white flour
- 12 oz lard
- 1 teaspoon salt
- 8 fl oz water

The filling
- 2 lbs fresh belly-pork (proportions two thirds lean to one third fat)
- 1 teaspoon anchovy essence
- 1 teaspoon salt
- ½ teaspoon ground white pepper

The jelly
- Bones, skin and gristly bits from the pork or (if you must) ready-made aspic

and pack it into the case, pressing well down. Roll out the smaller piece to lid the pie, damping the edges of the pastry, then press them together with a fork. Trim, make a hole in the top to let out the steam, decorate with pastry leaves, and glaze with a lick of beaten egg.

Bake at 200C/400F/Gas6 for 45 minutes. Reduce to 180C/350F/Gas4 and bake for 1 ½–2 hours, until the pastry is firm and brown. Unmould if you've baked it inside the tin, and return to the oven for ten minutes to brown the sides. If the pie's free-standing, it'll have the bow-shape characteristic of the true Melton Mowbray. Congratulations.

Meanwhile, for the jelly, make a strong stock with the pig bits, strain and reduce to about ½ pint. Pour the broth into the steam-hole as soon as the pie comes out of the oven. Leave to cool and set. Pop it in your pocket and head for the hills.

Georgian shchi

A robust vegetable-and-mutton stew to mirror the ethnic mix in a Georgian marketplace (sketched above): Russian cabbage, Mediterranean vegetables and Turkish mountain sheep. The Georgians are of Viking stock and their yellow-haired, blue-eyed daughters were much prized by the Ottoman sultans. Serve with rye bread flavoured with caraway.

Serves 4–6

SALT THE CABBAGE and put it between two plates. Set the lamb riblets to fry gently in the oil in a flame-proof casserole. As soon as the fat runs and the meat begins to brown, add the onions and let them fry gently until soft and golden.

Push the meat and onions aside and add the aubergine. Let it fry gently. When the aubergines are softish, add the tomatoes, diced pumpkin and the wine and/or water. Bring the pot back to the boil, turn down the heat, lid loosely and let everything simmer for 40–60 minutes (or transfer to the oven at 180C/350F/Gas4) until the meat is quite tender. Check and add more boiling water if it looks like running dry. Rinse the salt off the cabbage and drop it on top of the stew, basting it with the oily juices. Lid again and cook for another 10 minutes, till the cabbage is tender.

Ingredients
- 1 small green firm-headed cabbage, finely shredded
- 1 lb stewing mutton or breast of lamb cut into riblets
- 1 tablespoon olive or seed oil
- 2 onions, skinned and finely sliced
- 2 aubergines, diced
- 1 lb plum tomatoes (fresh or canned)
- 1 thick slice pumpkin, skinned and diced
- 1 pint white wine and/or water
- Salt and pepper

Merchant Ivory's easy lamb curry

Film-maker Ismail Merchant contributed his own version of a quick curry to David Burnett and Helen Saberi's *The Road to Vindaloo* (Prospect, 2008). Enough for the audience of village ladies as well as cast and crew.

Serves 10–12

PLACE EVERYTHING in one layer in a large roasting tin and toss to combine.

Cook at 190C/375F/Gas5 for 1 ½ hours.

Meanwhile, make the accompanying rice.
Fry the onions in butter or ghee till golden. Add the cloves, cinnamon stick and cashews, season with a little salt, add the rice and simmer in water like risotto.

Ingredients

- 4-lb boneless leg of lamb, cubed
- 2 teaspoons fresh ginger, grated
- 3 green chillies, sliced with seeds
- 1 garlic clove, crushed
- 1 ½ tablespoons chopped coriander or parsley
- 1 tablespoon lemon juice
- 2 tablespoons runny honey
- 3 tablespoons water

The rice

- 1 ½ lbs long-grain rice (basmati, patna)
- 2–3 medium onions, finely sliced
- 4 tablespoons ghee or butter
- 4 cloves
- 1 short cinnamon stick
- 4 tablespoons toasted cashews
- Salt

Braised shoulder of lamb with potatoes and lemon

Sunday lunch by the sea in secluded Kale, Turkey (above) is a leisurely affair when the dish of the day can be left to cook overnight in the baker's cooling bread oven. Shoulder – rich meat with plenty of flavour, and fattier and harder to carve than the leg – is perfect for braising. Have your butcher chop the joint right through the bone to give 8–10 meaty chunks.

A 5-lb shoulder feeds 6

PREHEAT THE OVEN to 180C/350F/Gas4.

Arrange all the ingredients in a large roasting tin and mix thoroughly with your hands. Cover with foil and transfer to the oven. After an hour, remove the foil, baste everything with the lemony juices, and roast uncovered for another 30–40 minutes until the meat is tender, the potatoes deliciously tipped with brown, and the juice reduced to a fragrant little slick.

Serve with quartered lemons and a salad of mustardy leaves – rocket, watercress, chicory, frisée – for which the oily drippings will be sufficient dressing.

Ingredients

- 1 shoulder of lamb, robustly chunked
- About 8 tablespoons Greek virgin olive oil
- About 3 lbs medium-sized waxy potatoes, peeled and quartered
- 2 lemons, scrubbed and roughly chopped
- 6–7 garlic cloves, unskinned but halved
- 4–5 rosemary sprigs
- 1 tablespoon dried oregano (not that soft greenhouse stuff)
- 1 glass white wine
- Sea salt and cracked pepper (crack whole pepper corns in the mortar)

Slow-cooked lamb with almonds

An Easter dish from Seville, where the whole population lines the streets to observe the events of Holy Week with magnificent candlelit processions. Lamb cooked with almonds is seen as *comida moro*, Moorish food, though the inclusion of serrano ham marks it as *converso* – converted. Andalusia was under Muslim rule for seven centuries and both land and people keep the print.

Serves 4–6

WIPE OVER THE lamb steaks and season with salt and pepper. Toast the almonds gently in a heavy earthenware or enamel casserole with a teaspoon of oil; as soon as the skins loosen and the nuts begin to brown, remove and reserve.

Reheat the casserole with the remaining oil and fry the meat, turning to brown all sides. Add the garlic cloves and serrano ham and fry for another few minutes. Add the herbs, wine and a glass of water, and bubble up. Turn down the heat and leave to simmer gently, loosely lidded, for an hour, till the meat is tender enough to eat with a spoon. Or transfer to the oven and cook

at 160C/325F/Gas3 for the same amount of time. Check occasionally and add another glassful of water if necessary. The cooking broth should be well-reduced by the end, but the meat should never be allowed to dry out.

Remove a spoonful of the broth, add it to the reserved almonds and *pimentón*/paprika in the liquidiser (or use a pestle and mortar), and pound to a paste.

Stir the paste into the cooking juices and bubble up again to thicken. Heap everything on a warm serving dish and finish, if you like, with a handful of flaked toasted almonds.

Ingredients

- 3 lbs thick lamb steaks (shoulder or leg), chopped right across the bone
- 4 tablespoons whole unblanched almonds
- 4 tablespoons olive oil
- 1 tablespoon diced serrano ham
- 1 whole head garlic cloves (about a dozen), broken but not skinned
- 1–2 bay leaves and a thyme sprig
- 1 glass white wine or dry sherry
- 1 tablespoon *pimentón* (Spanish paprika, smoked for preference) or standard paprika
- Salt and pepper

Mutton Cutlets with Espagnole Sauce

'Cheffy' stuff for a special occasion, such as dining rich great-aunt Agatha or jockeying for position with a new girlfriend, says Pilot Officer William Fowler in *Countryman's Cooking* (first published shortly after World War Two and republished in 2006 by Excellent Press). 'The mutton cutlet,' he adds by way of explanation, 'has an innocent look on the plate, with an old-world charm and serenity that belies the black heart beating beneath the Savile Row jacket.'

Serves 2

'**CUTLETS ARE** rather small, and quite a lot of them is trimmed off, so be sure you buy enough,' says Fowler the countryman. 'Cut away all the fat, leaving the piece of lean at the top. Beat up an egg and dip the cutlet, which has already been very lightly dusted with flour, in it. Then roll it in breadcrumbs and fry for about five minutes on each side in olive oil. It should now have an attractive golden appearance. If it is still possible to get cutlet frills, the Good Old Days illusion would be heightened. Before you fried the cutlets you would have made some Espagnole sauce.

'To prepare the sauce, chop up 2 onions, 1 large carrot and 2 oz lean bacon. Fry them in 2 oz butter till they are a rich brown colour. Scatter in a heaped tablespoon of flour and fry till golden. Now add ½ pound tinned tomatoes, a glass of white wine and 1 ½ pints stock. Bring to the boil, stirring continuously. Add a bouquet garni consisting of parsley, thyme and bay leaf. Simmer without a lid for an hour, stirring now and again. Strain into a clean pan and simmer slowly for another half hour – and you've finished.'

Ingredients
- 6 mutton cutlets
- 1 large egg, forked to blend
- Seasoned flour for dusting
- Breadcrumbs for coating
- Olive oil for frying

The sauce
- 2 onions
- 1 large carrot
- 2 oz lean bacon
- 2 oz butter
- 1 heaped tablespoon flour
- 8 oz tinned tomatoes
- 1 glass white wine
- 1 ½ pints stock
- Bouquet garni

Greek Christmas pork

I sketched this fresco in the Orthodox Church belonging to the monastery on the Greek island of Patmos. Pork is the traditional Christmas meat in much of the Christian world. While the British got rid of the boar's head after the Reformation – pagan stuff, said Lord Protector Cromwell – the Greeks, Russians and the rest of Orthodox Christianity stuck with what they knew and loved. Which, since pig-meat in all its forms is prohibited for both Muslim and Jew, this might be said to make a point. The leg, shoulder and loin are all suitable joints for the Christmas roast.

Serves 8–10

ALLOW THE MEAT to come up to room temperature if it's been stored in the fridge: this is particularly important when dealing with a large piece of meat which, if chilled, can cause oven temperature to drop dramatically, making nonsense of the cooking time. Preheat the oven to 180C/350F/Gas4. Dry the joint very thoroughly with a clean cloth. Rub with oil, salt and pepper. Make slits near the bone and poke in the halved garlic cloves. Set the joint in a roomy roasting pan, cover with foil, shiny side down, and transfer to the oven. It'll take about 2 ½ hours in all, allowing 25 minutes per pound.

After the first hour, remove the foil and tuck the potatoes along-side the meat, adding a few sprigs of rosemary. Reduce the oven heat to 160C/325F/Gas3, and roast for another 1 ½ hours, till the meat juices run clear when you pierce the thickest part with a skewer. Baste everything regularly and reduce the heat a little further if it looks like burning.

> *Pork is the traditional Christmas meat in much of the Christian world. Which, since pig-meat in all its forms is prohibited for both Muslim and Jew, this might be said to make a point*

Meanwhile, make the sauce. Simmer the apricots with the raisins, spices, orange juice and zest, in just enough water to cover for 15–20 minutes, till the fruit is perfectly tender – or place in a closed pot in the oven if there's room. Fish out the spices, if you can find them. Transfer the joint to a warm serving dish and allow the meat to settle and firm for 20 minutes or so. Meanwhile, pour the apricot juices only into the roasting tin and bubble up, scraping in the sticky brown bits, then stir in the fruit. Serve the pork in thick slices, with the apricot sauce and potatoes.

Ingredients
- 6–7-lb pork joint on the bone (leg, shoulder or loin), skinned
- 3–4 garlic cloves, halved lengthwise
- 2–3 tablespoons olive oil
- 2–3 sprigs rosemary
- 4 lbs potatoes, peeled and chunked
- Salt and pepper

Apricot sauce
- 8 oz dried apricots
- 4 oz currants or raisins
- 1 well-scrubbed orange, juice and finely grated zest
- 3–4 cloves
- Short-length cinnamon stick

Tourte champenoise

A buttery puff-pastry double-crust pie, just right for a Mayday picnic. The first of May marks the start of the agricultural year in the cold lands of the north, and Flora's feast day was (and still is) celebrated with a picnic in the open air, providing lovers with an opportunity for a little courting. Field food must be portable and the wine plentiful.

Serves 2, generously

Ingredients
For the pastry
- 8 oz flour
- ½ teaspoon salt
- 1–2 tablespoons cold water
- 6 oz butter

For the filling
- 8 oz lean pork, sliced small
- 2–3 tablespoons dry white wine
- 1 egg
- 1 heaped tablespoon grated cheese
- ½ teaspoon nutmeg
- Salt and pepper

CHAMPAGNE DAWN

PUT THE SLICED PORK to marinate with the wine. Make sure everything is cold, including all the implements. See that the butter is firm without being hard. Sieve the flour with the salt. Using a knife (or the food processor), cut in a third of the butter until you have a mixture like fine breadcrumbs. Mix in enough water to make a paste. Work it a little until it doesn't stick to your fingers.

Set the dough aside for 20 minutes, with the rest of the butter beside it, so that pastry and butter both reach the same temperature.

Roll out the pastry to a thick-ness of a pound coin. Dot it with the butter, cut into small pieces the size of a hazelnut. Then fold the pastry into three, like a napkin. Roll it out and then fold it into three again in the opposite direction. Set aside for 20 minutes.

Go through the last process twice more, adding the same amount of butter each time. Set the pastry aside for 20 minutes after each process. Then leave it for another 20 minutes before using it.

Divide the pastry in half. Roll one piece out and use it to line a shallow pie dish. Roll out the remaining piece to make a lid.

Let the pastry rest for the last time while you make the filling.

Heat the oven to 190C/375F/ Gas 5. Whisk the egg with the grated cheese and season the meat with the nutmeg, salt and pepper. Spread the meat filling in the pie dish, topping it with the egg and cheese mixture. Dampen the pastry edges and cover the pie with the lid, pressing the edges closed with a fork. Make a steam-hole in the top.

Bake the pie for 45–50 minutes, turning down the heat if it browns too fast. Wrap it in cloth and tuck it in the basket – and don't forget the ice-bucket to chill the champagne.

Mutton pasties

You'll find variations on the pasty, the universal convenience food, among Carpathian shepherds as well as Cornish tin-miners (and, indeed, as a handy bite for commuters passing through Paddington station). Tidily enclosed in dough – so unlikely to fall to pieces in the pocket – it'll keep warm in a paper bag.

Makes 4 large pasties

FIRST PREPARE the filling. Slice the meat finely and cut the slices into small squares. Dice the potatoes and onion. Mix all together in a bowl and season with salt and pepper.

Sift the flour with the salt. Bring the water to the boil in a large pan with the fat – suet, butter or lard – and boil until it melts. Beat in the flour and cook until the paste comes away from the sides of the pan. This is a hot-water paste and will look slightly transparent. Tip it out onto a well-floured board, knead into a ball and cut into quarters. Work quickly before it cools and cracks. Roll each quarter into a circle as thick as a pound coin.

Preheat the oven to 180C/350F/Gas4.

Divide the meat mixture between each circle, piling it up in the middle. Dampen the edges of the pastry and pull them over the filling to meet in the middle. Pinch the edges together to make a wavy line, known as the Cornish crimp. Leave a little hole in the middle for escaping steam. Glaze with egg if you like a shiny crust. Bake for 50–60 minutes, till the pastry is crisp and brown.

Ingredients
The filling:
- 1 lb boned-out mutton or lamb
- 1 lb mature potatoes
- 1 small onion
- Salt and pepper

Pastry
- 1 lb flour
- ½ teaspoon salt
- 8 oz grated suet or butter or lard
- 4–5 tablespoons water

Sir Walter Scott's rare roast beef

If you roast your beef by Sir Walter's unusual but effective method, says Clarissa Dickson Wright, you'll get crisp fat and succulent meat with minimum fuss. The timings won't work with a joint of less than 5 lbs and can't be done in an Aga.

Serves 8–10

ALLOW THE MEAT to come up to room temperature: take it out of the fridge an hour before you mean to cook it. Heat the oven to maximum – 240C/475F/Gas 9 or thereabouts – for at least 20 minutes.

Smear the joint with butter or dripping and season it thoroughly. Place it on a rack over a dripping-pan and transfer to the oven. Roast at the high heat for 5 minutes per pound – a total of 40–50 minutes – then turn the oven off. Leave for 2 hours, resisting the temptation to open the door. At the end of the allotted time, open the oven and feel the meat with your fingertips. If it's hot, serve it. If it's lukewarm, reheat the oven to maximum and give it another 10–15 minutes.

Heat the plates, and hand your carver a sharp knife to carve the beef on the bone. Serve it with its own gravy, grated horseradish folded into whipped cream, Yorkshire pud flavoured with sage and thyme, and potatoes roasted in goose fat.

Ingredients
- 8–10-lb sirloin or forerib on the bone
- Home-made dripping or butter
- Salt and pepper

Marinade for tough venison

A classic marinade guaranteed to break down the chewiest wild meat. Leave it overnight, and next day proceed as for your favourite slow-cooked pot-roast, using the sieved marinade diluted with its volume of water as the cooking liquid.

Enough for a 3–4-lb boned-out joint

COMBINE ALL the ingredients. Slash the meat with a sharp knife to ensure the marinade penetrates deeply into the flesh (or use a syringe).

Place the meat and marinade in a plastic or glass or stainless steel container, cover and refrigerate overnight.

Ingredients
- ¼ pint red wine
- 3 tablespoons balsamic vinegar
- 2 tablespoons molasses or treacle
- 2 tablespoons thyme, chopped
- 2 tablespoons rosemary, chopped
- 1 tablespoon juniper berries, crushed
- 3 garlic cloves, minced
- Zest of 3 unwaxed oranges
- Zest of 3 unwaxed lemons
- 8 cloves
- 8 peppercorns
- 2 bay leaves
- ¾ teaspoon salt

55

Swedish tjälknöl

Salt your own moose from the wild lands of the north for the Christmas smörgåsbord, and serve it just as they like it in Vadholm in the Swedish region of Södermanlands Län – sliced very thinly, with Scandinavian crispbread. If you can't get moose – why ever not? – it works just as well with red deer venison.

Serves a couple of dozen smörgåsborders

PUT THE FROZEN joint in an ovenproof dish into which it just fits, and set the dish in a cold oven.

Turn the oven on to a very low setting, 80C/175F/Gas¼, and leave the joint in the oven for 12 hours. When you test it with a meat thermometer, the inside should read 65C/150F and the meat should still be pink.

Meanwhile, boil the water with the rest of the ingredients and allow them to cool completely.

Transfer the cooked joint into the cold liquid and leave it there for 5 hours. After this time, remove the meat from the brine and allow it to drain dry. Put it in a plastic bag in the fridge, or freeze it again for future use. Serve cold, very thinly sliced, with a cranberry compote and very thin crispbread. Good with a fennel salad, creamy potato gratin and a mustardy remoulade with dill.

Ingredients

- 4-lb chunk frozen boned-out venison (a large lump, not a skinny fillet)
- 2 pints water
- 4 oz sea salt
- 2 tablespoons sugar
- 1 bay leaf
- ½ teaspoon crushed black pepper
- 15 juniper berries, crushed (count 'em – you know how the Swedes like to get things right)

Chinese-style oxtail

Long gentle cooking in a closed pot – the earth-oven method, so convenient when you live in a tropical paradise such as Singapore – ensures that the meat is pull-apart tender and even the smallest pieces are coated in a rich anise-flavoured sauce, says Jennifer McLagan in *Cooking on the Bone* (Grub Street, 2008).

Serves 4

PREHEAT THE oven to 150C/300F/Gas2.

Season the oxtail and brown the pieces in batches in the oil in a flameproof casserole, transferring them to a plate as they brown. Discard the fat from the pot, add the wine and bubble up, scraping up the browned bits from the bottom. Mix the sugar with the soy sauce and add to the pot along with a pint of water, the star anise, spring onion, ginger, garlic, orange zest and the oxtail. Bring to the boil, cover with damp parchment, lid tightly, and transfer to the oven to cook gently for 1 1/2 hours. Turn the pieces in the juice, re-seal and return to the oven for 1 1/2 hours, till the oxtail is very tender. Remove and reserve the oxtail in a shallow oven-proof dish.

Sieve the juices, discarding the debris, and allow to cool, preferably overnight in the fridge.

Ingredients
- 5 lbs oxtail pieces, trimmed
- Sea salt and freshly ground pepper
- 2–4 tablespoons vegetable oil
- ¼ pint Chinese rice wine or dry sherry
- ¼ pint dark soy sauce
- 1 ½ tablespoons brown sugar
- 1 star anise, broken apart
- 3 spring onions, trimmed and chopped
- 4 thin slices fresh ginger
- 2 garlic cloves, chopped
- 1 orange, zest and juice

Lamb korma

In *Curry, a Biography* (Chatto, 2005) – a useful tome which accompanied me on my travels in Rajasthan in search of Mogul foodways a year or two ago – historian Lizzie Collingham ascribes the technique of tenderising tough meat by leaving it overnight in yoghurt to the cooks of the Mogul court, who learned the trick from the Persians. Something of a mix-and-match, spices were the Indian contribution, cream was added as an enrichment by the chefs of Lucknow, while chillis, a New World import, were introduced to India by the Portuguese. Fancy that, as the ladies of Kakelaw might say.

Serves 4–5

HEAT THE OIL in a pan and add the cinnamon, cardamom, cloves and bay leaves. Stir in the hot oil for 30 seconds. Turn down the heat and add the onions. Fry, stirring, for 5 minutes. Remove from the heat and allow to cool. Stir in the yoghurt and mix in the lamb and the ground almonds. Cover and leave overnight in the fridge.

Remove the meat from the fridge and allow it to come up to room temperature. Heat the oil in a pan and fry the ginger, garlic and chillis for about 10 minutes. Add the spices and stir over the heat for a minute. Add the meat and its marinade and fry fiercely for another minute. Add salt and a teaspoon of sugar. Lid and simmer gently for 30 minutes or so, till the lamb is perfectly tender. You may need to add a little water. Stir in the cream and simmer uncovered for another 10 minutes.

Ingredients
- 1 ½ lbs diced, boned lamb
- 3 tablespoons vegetable oil
- 1 short-length cinnamon stick
- 10 cardamom pods
- 10 whole cloves
- 2 bay leaves
- 1 large onion, finely chopped
- 2 oz ground almonds
- 6 tablespoons plain yoghurt

The sauce
- 4–6 tablespoons vegetable oil
- Nugget fresh ginger, finely grated
- 6 garlic cloves, crushed
- 2 green chillis, finely chopped
- 1 teaspoon powdered coriander
- 1 teaspoon powdered cumin
- ½ teaspoon garam masala
- Salt and a little sugar
- ¼ pint single cream

KAKELAW

Sosaties

This is the Boer version of Indonesia's satay sticks. Early settlers in the Cape ate their way through the zebra population of southern Africa, imported (to put it delicately) their domestic servants from the Dutch colonies, and sensibly adopted Indonesian culinary habits as preferable to their own.

Serves 4–6

TRIM THE LAMB, reserving the fat and cutting it into fine slivers, and chop the meat into bite-sized pieces.

Bring all the marinade ingredients to the boil in a small saucepan, stir, turn down the heat and simmer for 5 minutes. Allow to cool, then mix well with the meat in a bowl. Cover and leave to marinate in the fridge overnight – 3 days is better, 5 is perfect.

Drain the meat and thread it on skewers, alternating with slivers of fat. If using bamboo satay-sticks, soak them first.

Lay the sosaties on the barbecue – the heat should be high and smokeless. Turn them once. They should be charred on the outside but tender and juicy within.

Serve with satay sauce – if anyone has a peanut allergy, make it with walnuts or almonds or pecans. To prepare, whizz up all the sauce ingredients in a liquidiser, bring to the boil in a small pan and stir over the heat until the cornflour cooks and thickens the sauce a little.

Bread and kachoomer – a scooping salad of chopped tomatoes, onions and chilli dressed with lemon juice and cumin – will keep the punters happy while the *braai* gets under way.

Ingredients
- 1 boned-out shoulder of lamb (zebra being off the menu)

The marinade
- 1 glass red wine
- 4 tablespoons wine vinegar
- 2 garlic cloves, skinned and sliced
- A few bruised lemon leaves or 1 tablespoon lemon zest
- 3 tablespoons curry powder (Bolst's for preference)
- 1 tablespoon brown sugar
- 1 tablespoon ground allspice
- 1 teaspoon ground cardamom
- 1 teaspoon salt

Satay sauce
- ½ pint coconut milk
- 3 tablespoons peanut butter (rough rather than smooth)
- 1 teaspoon cornflour
- 1 teaspoon ground cumin
- 1 teaspoon ground chilli
- 1 tablespoon grated fresh ginger
- 1 tablespoon soy sauce
- A splash of dry sherry or white wine

Marguerite Patten's pressure-cooked blanquette of veal

Eat up your veal, do the dairy farmer a favour and save our boy calves from meeting the inevitable in faraway places. Marguerite Patten gives this classic way with stewing veal in a welcome reprint of *The Basic Basics Pressure Cooker Cookbook* (Grub Street, 2010). A blanquette is light, summery and reheatable, and the meat is a lot more interesting than chicken.

Serves 4

FRY THE MEAT and onions in the butter in the open cooker for 1–2 minutes. Do not brown. Add the stock, bouquet garni and seasoning, cook for 12 minutes at H/15 lb pressure, then reduce the pressure so you can open the lid. Remove the bouquet garni, blend the flour with half the milk or cream, add to the stock and stir over a low heat until thickened.

Blend the rest of the milk or cream, egg yolk(s) and lemon juice, whisk into the hot sauce, and heat gently for 2–3 minutes.

Serve with plain white rice. To cook white rice for 4 in a pressure cooker, you'll need 2 teacups filled to the brim with long-grain rice. Put 4 teacups of water into the cooker, add ½ teaspoon of salt, bring the water to the boil and add the rice. Stir briskly, fix the cover and bring to H/25 lb pressure. Lower the heat and cook for 5 minutes. Reduce the pressure under cold water. Spread the rice on a hot dish, put into a pre-heated oven, turn off the oven and leave the rice to dry in the residual heat.

Ingredients
- 1 ½ lbs stewing veal, cut into neat fingers
- 2 lbs onions, sliced
- Generous half pint white stock
- Bouquet garni (thyme, bay, parsley stalks)
- Salt and pepper
- 1 oz plain flour
- ¼ pint milk or single cream
- 1 or 2 egg yolks
- 1 tablespoon lemon juice

Chapter 4
Poultry & Game

Barnyard birds – chickens and ducks – have been kept as egg-layers since the earliest times. To our self-sufficient farming ancestors, there had to be a very good reason to kill a productive egg-layer for meat. Which left chicken, a tender young bird fattened up for the spit, the food of the rich.

Chicken didn't become the cheapest meat on the slab until the introduction of intensive poultry-rearing during World War Two, when poultry meat was used as a fall-back protein source to carry us through the shortages of the war. Until then, few of us could afford to eat an egg-producer – ducks as well as hens – until she was past her laying-days and fit for nothing but the boiling-pot. Victorian household manuals emphasise the need to tenderise an old hen by long gentle cooking, before stripping the meat from the carcass for inclusion in pies and puddings. And in the days when cock-fighting was a popular spectator sport, the same treatment was allotted the sinewy carcasses of birds toughened up for their appearance in the ring. Of these, Scotland's cock-a-leekie and France's coq-au-vin are the most obvious survivors.

The medieval menu favoured feathered game – heron, bittern and crane, as well as grouse and partridge – and paid little attention to barnyard birds. Game birds, particularly the non-native pheasant, were always the privilege of the land-owner, while more modest households might fatten up a capon or two in the barnyard for a wedding feast.

> *To our self-sufficient farming ancestors, there had to be a very good reason to kill a productive egg-layer for meat. Which left chicken, a tender young bird, the food of the rich*

By Victorian times, grandees with vast estates in the provinces and lavish lifestyles to support in the city, had poultry and game baked in enormous pies and sent up from country to town. The festive bird of the autumn and winter feasts was goose, a strictly seasonal breeder which comes to market in its first year from September till Christmas, while turkey, a New World native, has only been the Christmas bird since about the end of the nineteenth century.

Circassian pheasant

A sophisticated dish, said to have been introduced to the Ottoman sultan by a Georgian princess, which combines pheasant, a game bird native to the Caucasus, with a Turkish walnut sauce spiced with cinnamon. You can make it with chicken or any other game bird, and almonds or hazelnuts can replace the walnuts.

Serves 4–6

WIPE OVER THE pheasants and singe off any stray feathers.

Settle the birds in a roomy pan with the pot-herbs, salt, peppercorns and enough water to cover. Bring to the boil, turn down the heat, lid loosely and leave to simmer for about 1 ½ hours. Don't let the pot return to the boil or the meat will be stringy. Remove the birds when perfectly tender. Skin and de-bone, cut the meat into bite-sized pieces and reserve. Return the bones to the broth and bubble up till reduced to about a pint. Strain the broth and reserve.

Meanwhile, dry-roast the walnuts in a heavy pan for a few minutes until lightly toasted – don't let them burn (10 minutes in the oven will do the trick). Drop the nuts and the rest of the sauce ingredients into the processor with a ladleful of the chicken broth. Process to a thick purée, then thin it with the remaining broth. Turn the pheasant pieces in the sauce, pile on a dish and trickle with the oil mixed with the chilli.

Serve at room temperature with white rice tossed with pomegranate seeds, if in season.

Ingredients

- 2 pheasants
- 1 onion, quartered
- 1 carrot, roughly chopped
- A few parsley stalks
- Salt and peppercorns

For the sauce

- 6 tablespoons freshly shelled walnuts, skinned
- 3 rounded tablespoons fresh white breadcrumbs
- 1 garlic clove, skinned and roughly chopped
- 1 teaspoon powdered cinnamon
- Salt and pepper

To finish

- 1–2 tablespoons walnut or olive oil
- ½ teaspoon powdered chilli

A sophisticated dish, said to have been introduced to the Ottoman sultan by a Georgian princess. Serve at room temperature with white rice tossed with pomegranate seeds

Ethiopian chicken curry

Delicately spiced and fiery with chilli, *doro wett*, chicken stew, is the dish traditionally served at weddings or festivals – such as St George's Day (above) – in Ethiopia. It's eaten with a scooping-bread, *injeera*, a big floppy crumpet-like flatbread made by pouring a leavened batter onto a hot bakestone (see recipe page 153).

The traditional *injeera* flour is teff, a tiny primitive grain never altered by cultivation which, when pounded and mixed with water, produces its own built-in yeasts and develops its own digestive enzymes. The flavour of *injeera* is sour, a little beery and oddly addictive, and is usually eaten with small amounts of assorted *wett* – stew – of which the everyday version, as in India, is based on a variety of pulses and seasonal vegetables. The two elements, *wett* and *injeera*, when served together, are flagged on Ethiopia's tourist menus as 'Assorted National Foods'. Failing *injeera*, a *wett* can be eaten with Italianate white bread rolls (a result of Italian occupation in World War Two) or any other scooping-breads, such as Indian chapatis or Middle Eastern pittas.

Serves 6–8

SKIN THE CHICKEN joints, rub with quartered lime and transfer to a bowl with the ginger, chilli and spices. Turn to mix well, cover and reserve.

Heat a heavy saucepan, add the diced onion and cook very gently till the onion begins to soften. Continue to cook till the onion is perfectly soft and golden brown – no oil or butter, though you can add a little water if it threatens to burn.

Add the butter and heat till it oils. Add the chicken pieces, garlic and diced red pepper, and stir over the heat. Add the wine and the spicy juices from the chicken and bubble up. Add enough water to barely cover the meat, bubble up again, turn down the heat, lid loosely and simmer gently for 30–40 minutes, till the onions are completely melted and the meat is almost dropping off the bone. Add a little salt and bubble up until the sauce is thick and shiny. Taste and adjust the seasoning.

Serve on (or with) a scooping-bread and any other vegetable curry, hard-boiled eggs, a dish of plain-cooked dhal and a dish of yoghurt or soft curd-cheese to cool the palate.

Ingredients

- 1 small free-range chicken, jointed small
- 1 lime, roughly chopped
- 1 small piece fresh ginger, finely chopped
- 1 tablespoon chilli flakes
- ½ teaspoon ground cardamom
- ½ teaspoon coarsely ground black pepper
- 3 pints diced red onions
- 6 oz unsalted butter
- 2 garlic cloves, chopped
- ½ pint diced red pepper
- ¼ pint red wine

Poached chicken with prunes and cream

A Yorkshire dish known as Hindle Wakes – 'hen de la wake' or 'chicken-in-mourning' (wake up there at the back) – which was traditionally prepared during Easter week and eaten in the early hours of Easter Sunday when people returned home from church after the fasting vigil of the Eve.

Serves 6–8

WIPE OVER THE chicken and season it inside and out. Pit the prunes (drain them if they were soaked overnight). Melt half the butter (grate the rest) in a small frying pan, add the finely chopped onion and fry till soft and golden. Stir in the breadcrumbs, parsley and the juice and zest of one lemon. Remove from the heat and work in the grated butter. Stuff the pitted prunes with the mixture, arrange in a buttered baking dish and cover with foil.

Bake at 180C/350F/Gas4 for 25 minutes, remove and allow to cool.

Meanwhile, pack the bird, neatly trussed, into a pot just large enough to contain it. Add the vinegar, carrot, onion, salt and pepper and just enough water to cover the thighs of the bird well (the breasts will cook in the steam).

Cover with a tight-fitting lid and cook gently on top of the stove for about 45 minutes, or until the thighs are tender: add more boiling water if necessary to keep up the level. Leave to cool for an hour in the cooking liquor.

Remove the bird, skin it and cut into nice serving portions, taking out any bones. Arrange the pieces on a dish. Cover with foil so the meat doesn't dry out, but let it get quite cold. Don't refrigerate unless absolutely necessary. Skim as much fat off the liquor as possible, and measure out 1 ½ pints of the broth, pouring it through a sieve.

Now make the sauce. Melt the butter in a pan, stir in the flour and gradually work in the measured broth, whisking to avoid lumps. Cook for 10 minutes, stirring throughout, till smooth and reduced by a third. Stir in the juice and zest of the remaining lemon, taste and adjust the seasoning.

Transfer to a bowl and cover the surface with oiled paper to prevent a skin forming as the sauce cools. Lightly whip the cream and fold it into the cold sauce.

Coat each piece of chicken with the sauce. Finish with the stuffed prunes, watercress and quartered lemons.

You can, if you wish, serve the chicken warm by reheating it carefully in its sauce.

> *A Yorkshire dish known as Hindle Wakes –*
> *'hen de la wake' or 'chicken-in-mourning' –*
> *which was traditionally prepared during Easter*
> *week and eaten in the early hours of Easter Sunday*

Ingredients
- A large roasting chicken (about 5 lbs dressed weight)
- 1 lb ready-to-eat prunes (if dried, soak overnight in strong hot tea)
- 2 oz butter
- 1 small onion, finely chopped
- 2 heaped tablespoons fresh breadcrumbs
- 1 tablespoon chopped parsley
- 2 lemons, juice and finely grated zest
- 2 large carrots, scraped and chunked
- 1 large onion, chunked
- ¼ pint red wine vinegar
- Salt and pepper

For the sauce
- 2 oz butter
- 2 tablespoons plain flour
- ¼ pint double cream

To serve
- A big bunch of watercress
- Quartered lemons

67

Constance Spry's roast turkey with chestnut stuffing

Anyone in search of culinary common sense need look no further than *The Constance Spry Cookery Book* (Grub Street reprint, 2004). You may, if you wish, stuff the turkey cavity with sausage meat, says Mrs Spry, though my advice would be to slip chunks of lemon and onion inside and leave it at that. If you choose a solid stuffing, the bird will take longer, so calculate the weight once stuffed.

Serves 8–12

WIPE OVER THE TURKEY and season it inside and out.

Now prepare the stuffing: simmer the chopped prunes in the wine till tender, allowing the juice to reduce to 3–4 tablespoons. Fry the celery and onion in the butter till soft. Add the prunes (not the juice), herbs, lemon rind and chestnuts broken into pieces. Stir lightly with a fork, season well, then add the prune juice. When thoroughly cool, stir in the egg. Push the stuffing under the breast-flap, between the meat and the skin. Skewer into place.

Preheat the oven to 180C/350F/Gas4 and set the fat to melt in a roasting tin, which should be large enough to hold the turkey comfortably and leave room to baste easily. The fat should cover the bottom of the tin to a depth of 1 inch.

Cover the bird with buttered paper and put it in the oven. Roast, allowing approximately 10 minutes to the pound, and basting every 15–20 minutes. Take the paper off while doing so and replace it, until the last half-hour, when it may be removed for the final browning.

Turn the bird over fairly frequently during the roasting to ensure that the legs get a thorough cooking, and as much of the top heat as possible. So often the breast of a turkey, and particularly that of a large bird, gets stringy and overcooked, while the legs remain underdone. This can be avoided by cooking the bird for a greater part of the time on its side and turning it over as described.

Ingredients
- 1 medium-sized turkey, about 10–12 lbs
- Good beef dripping

Stuffing
- 12 large prunes, stoned and chopped
- ½ pint red wine
- 1 oz butter
- 1 small head celery, diced
- 2 tablespoons finely chopped onion
- 1 heaped teaspoon chopped mixed dried herbs
- Grated rind ½ lemon
- 8 oz cooked, skinned chestnuts
- Salt and pepper
- 1 small egg, forked to blend

Southern-fried chicken

Mark Twain sighed for it, Scarlett O'Hara almost died for it, and fried chicken brings tears to the eyes of every homesick Confederate – the ones who came second at the Battle of Gettysburg. Delicious hot, and just as good cold.

Serves 6 – more if you make plenty of chips

JOINT THE CHICKEN into 12 pieces. I use a hammer to tap a heavy knife straight through the bone.

Beat the egg and the milk lightly together in a deep plate.

Mix the breadcrumbs with the herbs on another plate.

Put the flour, salt, pepper, paprika and cayenne in a plastic or paper bag and give it a shake. Drop in the chicken pieces and shake them around to coat them in the seasoned flour.

Dip each floured chicken joint into the egg-and-milk and then press it well into the herby bread-crumbs. Make sure each piece is really well jacketed.

Heat the oil in a deep frying pan. When it is hot and lightly blue-hazed, put in the dark meat first. Fry for 5 minutes, then add the white meat.

The joints will need about 20 minutes of gentle frying – test with a skewer to make sure the juices run clear. If they are still a little pink when the coating is crisp and browned, transfer the pieces, well drained, to a moderate oven to finish cooking for 10 minutes or so.

Serve with a tomato sauce with enough chilli stirred into it to give it bite.

Ingredients

- 1 free-range chicken
- 1 large egg
- 1 small teacup milk
- 2 big handfuls home-made fresh breadcrumbs
- 1 tablespoon finely chopped parsley
- 1 tablespoon finely chopped thyme
- 1 teaspoon finely chopped sage
- 2–3 heaped tablespoons plain flour
- 1 teaspoon salt
- 1 teaspoon freshly milled black pepper
- 1 tablespoon paprika and a pinch of cayenne
- Oil for deep frying

Barbadian chicken yassa

Originally a recipe from Senegal, chicken yassa is a popular dish in Barbados (above) – a little taste of Caribbean sunshine. This version is from culinary expert Rosamund Grant, who was born in Barbados. The sharpness of the lemon becomes more mellow as the dish cooks, says Rosamund, and tastes even better the next day.

Serves 4–6

PUT THE CHICKEN joints in a roomy bowl with the onions, lemon juice, vinegar and 2 tablespoons of the oil. Leave to marinate for a few hours – overnight is even better.

Remove the chicken and onions and reserve the marinade. Grill the chicken joints on both sides till brown. Meanwhile fry the onions in the remaining oil for a few minutes, then add the reserved marinade, thyme, chilli, water or stock and the bay leaves, and simmer for 10 minutes. Slip the chicken into the sauce and simmer for approximately 35 minutes, till cooked through. Serve West Indian-style with boiled green bananas, plantains or mashed yam – better still, with a sweet potato mash (see page 108).

Ingredients
- 1 small free-range chicken, jointed and washed
- 3–4 medium onions, finely sliced
- 10 tablespoons lemon juice
- 4 tablespoons malt vinegar
- 4 tablespoons groundnut or sunflower oil
- 1 sprig thyme
- Chilli pepper to taste
- 1 pint water or stock
- 2 bay leaves

Saffron chicken for Norooz

The Zoroastrian New Year, Norooz – a festival of Ancient Persian origin – is celebrated wherever the sandy desert blooms or nations follow Islam. While the actual event is scheduled somewhat later than Christian Christmas and marks the start of spring, the form it takes has a great deal in common with our own midwinter festivals. Re-birth is the general thrust, with attention paid to the ancestral hearth-fires and the cycle of life and death, without which the world will end – as well it might, the world being what it is.

Here, in the interests of world peace and heavenly understanding, is a slice of Norooz cooking from *Persia in Peckham* by Sally Butcher (Prospect, 2007). Weigh the chicken when stuffed and allow 15 minutes per pound, plus 20 minutes extra for the warm-up.

Serves 6–8

SEASON THE INSIDE of the chicken with salt and pepper and set it in a roomy roasting tray.

Preheat the oven to 180C/350F/Gas4.

Drain the soaked fruit and pat or shake dry. Melt half the butter in a small pan and fry the fruit and nuts together, stirring well, for 6–7 minutes. Add the cinnamon, cardamom, cranberries/raisins and tomato purée and bubble up. Remove from the heat.

Cram the stuffing inside the chicken, folding over the flap of skin (or stitch up the opening) to hold it in place. Melt the rest of the butter, add the saffron and its soaking water, and drizzle this over the skin of the bird.

Cover with foil and roast in the oven for 40–50 minutes, till the chicken is nearly done.

Meanwhile, sauté the potato chips in a little oil and butter until they're golden. Remove the foil from the bird, baste it with juices, dot the potatoes round the side and return the tray to the oven for another 25–30 minutes at 190C/375F/Gas5, until the potatoes are cooked through and the bird's skin is golden and crisp.

Ingredients
- 1 large free-range chicken, 5–6 lbs dressed weight
- 2 tablespoons pre-soaked dried barberries (or sultanas)
- 6–8 prunes, soaked and pitted
- 6–8 dried apricots or peaches, soaked and roughly chopped
- 5 oz butter
- 2 tablespoons pitted sour cherries or pomegranate seeds
- 2 tablespoons roughly chopped walnuts
- 2 tablespoons roughly chopped almonds and/or pistachios
- 1 teaspoon ground cinnamon
- ½ teaspoon ground cardamom
- 1 tablespoon tomato purée
- 2 tablespoons cranberries or raisins
- 1 teaspoon powdered saffron, dissolved in 1 tablespoon boiling water
- 3 lbs potatoes, peeled and chipped
- Salt and pepper

> *Re-birth is the general thrust of Norooz, with attention paid to ancestral hearth-fires and the cycle of life and death, without which the world will end*

Sugar-brined butter-roast Thanksgiving turkey

The turkey in the wild, as observed in the woods of Maine not far from where the Pilgrim Fathers staked their claim, is perfectly patterned to match its surroundings. The males shine in bronze with silver-blue trim, the females shimmer in herring-bone tweed the colour of autumn. Now you see 'em, now you don't. A poll conducted by Boston-based *Saveur* magazine says that eighty per cent of all American households agree that the Thanksgiving turkey is all the better for a night in the brine-bucket. And since the turkey's a New World native, who are we to disagree?

A 10–12-lb bird serves 8–10

TOAST 2 TABLESPOONS of the sage leaves in a dry pan for 2 minutes. Add 1 lb sea salt, 8 oz sugar and about 4 pints of water. Transfer to a bowl or bucket large enough to accommodate the whole bird, *sans* giblets and well-wiped. Set in a cool place overnight or for at least 8 hours.

Preheat the oven to 180C/350F/Gas4.

Drain the bird and pat it dry. For ease of carving, remove the wishbone. Tuck the wings under the body and place the bird breast-up on a roasting rack set in a roomy baking tray. Paint the skin all over with melted butter and season with freshly ground pepper.

Make sure the bird is at room temperature before you put it in the oven. Roast for 2 ½–3 hours, basting whenever you remember. Reduce the oven to 170C/325F/Gas3 after the first hour. Test for doneness by pushing a skewer into the thickest part of the thigh – if the juices run clear, it's done. Leave to settle for at least 20 minutes before carving.

Sauce with its own juices bubbled up with a little brandy diluted with giblet stock: taste to make sure it's well seasoned and whisk in a spoonful of cream.

Traditional accompaniments are collard greens (shredded turnip tops or cabbage dressed with diced bacon, butter, vinegar, molasses and chilli); cornbread (soda bread in which half the flour is replaced with fine-ground cornmeal, including butter and an egg to hold the mixture together), roasted sweet potato (chunk and roast under the turkey), cranberry sauce (pop fresh berries in water with sugar).

A spoonful of breadcrumbs crisped in butter adds texture to the plateful – New Worlders find the British taste for bread sauce incomprehensible. Enjoy.

Ingredients
- 1 smallish free-range turkey
- 2–3 sprigs dried sage
- 1 lb sea salt
- 8 oz sugar

To roast
- 8 oz unsalted butter, melted
- Freshly ground pepper

Potted grouse and squirrel with juniper and nutmeg

This recipe is suitable for any elderly game of smallish size, whether feathered or furred. Candidates for the treatment are grouse, pheasant, partridge, duck, pigeon, rabbit, rook, squirrel, chicken, guinea fowl. If the birds are still in feather, skin and don't bother to pluck.

Serves 6–8

JOINT EVERYTHING roughly, rinse well and pack into a roomy pan with the peppercorns, juniper berries, sea salt and Worcestershire sauce. Add a scraping of nutmeg and enough water to cover. Bring to the boil, lid tightly, turn down the heat and simmer for about 1 ½ hours, until the meat is very soft, adding boiling water whenever the stock level drops below the meat.

Strip the meat from the bones and chop very finely. Return the bones to the pan with the stock and bubble up uncovered until reduced to ½ pint. Strain the stock into the meat, beat in the butter or lard, taste and adjust the seasoning. Pack into earthenware pots or jars, leave to cool and float a layer of melted butter or lard over the top. Good for 2 weeks in the fridge. Serve with melba toast, rhubarb chutney and pickled onions.

Ingredients
- About 6 lbs mixed game, gutted and skinned
- 1 teaspoon peppercorns
- 1 teaspoon juniper berries
- 1 teaspoon sea salt
- 1 teaspoon Worcestershire sauce
- ½ teaspoon freshly grated nutmeg
- 2–3 tablespoons butter or freshly made pork lard

To seal
- More butter or lard

Rabbit in red wine with olives and mushrooms

An easy way with game, just as they like it northern Italy. Serve with soft polenta and a dollop of soured cream.

Serves 4–6

RINSE THE JOINTS thoroughly. Transfer them to a bowl with the oil and lemon juice, thyme and bay, and leave for an hour or two to take the flavours.

Remove the joints and pat them dry, reserving the marinade, and flip them through seasoned flour. Heat the oil in a roomy casserole and fry the joints till they take a little colour. Push them aside and add the pancetta or bacon, garlic, carrot, mushrooms, and fry for another few minutes. Add the reserved marinade, the olives and wine and bubble up.

Turn down the heat, season with a little salt and plenty of pepper, lid tightly and simmer gently, or transfer to a low oven for 1–2 hours, till the meat is very soft. Check and add water if it looks like drying out. Remove the bones or not, as you please. Bubble up the juices till shiny and thick.

Ingredients

- 2–3 wild rabbits, jointed
- 2–3 tablespoons lemon juice
- 2–3 sprigs thyme
- 1–2 bay leaves
- A little flour
- 4 tablespoons olive oil
- 2 tablespoons diced pancetta or bacon
- 2–3 garlic cloves, crushed and chopped
- 1 large carrot, scraped and diced
- 3–4 large mushrooms (porcini, if you can get 'em), trimmed and sliced
- 2 tablespoons black olives
- 1 bottle robust red wine
- Salt and pepper

Pheasant chitamee

This is what Clarissa Dickson Wright's grandmother's second husband, Ezekial Manesseh, a member of the Sephardic community of Calcutta, did with a brace of elderly birds. And very good it is too.

Serves 4–6

COOK THE ONIONS gently in the oil until golden. Add the garlic, ginger, turmeric, coriander, cardamom and chillies and cook a little longer. Add the pheasant joints to the pan and sauté, turning them occasionally, for about 20 minutes.

Add the tomatoes and vinegar and cook for 30 minutes until the pheasant is well coated and the sauce is not too runny. If the dish is too sharp you may need to add a pinch of sugar.

A great dish for a party. Serve with rice, says Ms Dickson Wright, never a woman to waste words.

A side dish of thick plain yoghurt stirred with a handful of finely chopped spring onions would not come amiss.

> *This is what Clarissa Dickson Wright's grandmother's second husband, a member of the Sephardic community of Calcutta, did with a brace of elderly birds*

Ingredients

- 6 onions, finely chopped
- 3 tablespoons olive oil
- 3 garlic cloves, crushed
- Small piece ginger, finely chopped
- 1 teaspoon ground turmeric
- 1 tablespoon chopped coriander leaves or 1 teaspoon ground coriander seeds
- 6 green cardamom pods or 1 teaspoon ground cardamom
- 1–2 red chillies, finely chopped
- 2 pheasants, jointed
- 1 middle-sized can chopped tomatoes
- 2 tablespoons wine vinegar
- Salt and pepper

Boned stuffed poussins à la Marquis de Sade

This recipe (somewhat bowdlerised for useability) is one I particularly enjoyed from Mark Crick's delightful *Kafka's Soup* (originally published by Libri in 2005, reprinted in paperback by Granta in 2007), a literary fantasy billed as a complete history of world literature in 17 recipes. The heroine of the story, a luscious young virgin locked in the larder among boxes of low-sodium milk and vegetarian paté, describes the old ravisher's activities as observed through the keyhole: 'The judge [the Marquis' alter ego] was slowly peeling away the wrapping to reveal two fleshy white birds, breasts uppermost. I saw his eyes widen and he began talking to the two poussins. "What have we here? Two naughty little birds." As he spoke he gave one of them a playful slap. "We will need to teach you a lesson."' And so on – I'm sure you get the picture.

Serves 2 (of course)

BONE THE POUSSINS, using a sharp knife and your own interpretation of bird anatomy. Or have the butcher do the business for you.

Melt all but a tablespoon of the butter in a small pan. Fry the onion over a low heat till it softens, add the sliced mushrooms and chopped parsley and fry for another few minutes.

Work the contents of the pan with the rest of the stuffing ingredients, seasoning with salt and pepper. Divide the stuffing between the two carcasses, pushing it well into the breasts and working it up the drumsticks.

Sew up all the openings with button-thread, and pat, as the Marquis would have it, the brutalised creatures back into shape.

Melt the rest of the butter in a pan large enough to take the poussins side by side, but don't put them in yet. Toss in the chopped vegetables and turn them over the heat to brown.

Then put in the poussins, stock and bay leaf. Bring to the boil, reduce the heat, lid loosely and leave to simmer gently for 40–60 minutes, till the birds feel firm to the finger and their juices no longer run pink. Check every now and again and add more water if needed.

Remove the poussins to a serving dish and keep them warm in the oven. Push the remaining debris through a sieve to extract the juice, return the juice to the pan and bubble up till it achieves the consistency of runny honey.

Eat with your fingers – so handy for licking off the juices.

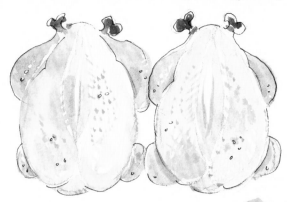

Ingredients
- 2 fat little poussins

The stuffing
- 3 oz butter
- 1 large onion, finely chopped
- A dozen button mushrooms, sliced
- 2 tablespoons finely chopped parsley
- 2 heaped tablespoons fresh white breadcrumbs
- Grated zest of ¼ lemon
- 3–4 ready-soaked prunes, stoned and diced
- 2–3 ready-soaked dried apricots, diced
- Salt and freshly ground pepper
- ½ a beaten egg

The poaching broth
- 6 tablespoons chopped onion, carrot, turnip and celery
- ½ pint chicken stock
- 1 bay leaf

Chapter 5
Pasta & Grains

rain-foods – rice, pasta and the rest of that merry band of seed-foods you'll find on the shelves of any whole-food store – provide most of the world with its daily diet. Storable, nutritious and easy to prepare, convenience foods made even more convenient by processing to reduce their cooking time, pasta and rice are now as widely available in our supermarkets as were rolled oats and pearl barley when we all bought our groceries from a real shopkeeper in the high street. And if you don't want to cook, you'll find them bulking out the ready-meals so many of us take home to pop in the microwave.

Traditionally, grain-foods have never been much more than a meat-stretcher in the British kitchen. Until, that is, the arrival of a cookbook which was so influential, so universally popular, that people changed the way they cooked. One such was the work of Isabella Beeton – poor young thing, dead before she was thirty – whose *Household Management* arrived at a time when our towns and cities, bloated by the workers of the industrial revolution, were filling up with aspirational young matrons who could afford servants, few of whom had any idea of what to do. Suddenly everyone began to do what granny never did – follow recipes and send out for take-aways (pie shops, mostly), leading to the disappearance of much of what was truly regional, a lack of interest in locally grown food, and a loss of understanding of what raw materials ought to taste like.

And then came World War Two, and just when we'd got the hang of cabbage-patch cooking and were beginning to rediscover the taste of a home-grown carrot and the joys of parsley sauce, along came Elizabeth David and – whoops – off we went again, skipping merrily down the road which led to pizza parlours and to a taste for watery tomatoes grown in Dutch glass-houses. Which, in turn, led – thanks to an appetite for travel and the arrival of immigrants who opened cook-shops and cheap eateries to feed those who couldn't afford an apartment with a kitchen – to an increasing awareness of what happens in the rest of the world.

This led, in the fullness of time, to the arrival in our shops of an avalanche of exotic ingredients – fresh root-ginger, hundreds of different chillis, lemongrass, fresh coriander, grains of paradise, Chinese star anise. Which prompted the popularising of dishes borrowed from the traditions of the Mediterranean, Middle East and Asia which combine grain-foods and pulses with fresh vegetables, dropping the need for meat as the centrepiece of a meal and shifting it into a subsidiary role as a flavouring ingredient, or even, thanks to the rising number of vegetarians among us, leaving it out altogether. Which then leads, as these things must, down the rocky road to ready-made pasta sauces and egg-fried rice from the cook-chill cabinet.

Catalan pasta paella

The Catalan *fideu* is made in much the same way as the Valencian paella, but with small pasta shapes rather than rice. The pasta element can be broken-up spaghetti or short macaroni or vermicelli or any small soup pasta, such as *lluvia* – rain – which is popular with children. The cooking instrument is identical to the paella pan – a round, shallow two-handled pan of Roman design – and there is no real difference in the method of preparation: the preliminary frying of the grain-food with its raw flavouring ingredients is followed by the addition of a cooking-liquid. The juices, however, are given a final thickening with the Catalan *picada*, a garlicky finishing mix of breadcrumbs crisped in oil with or without the addition of almonds.

Serves 6–8

Ingredients
- 10 oz rice-shaped pasta
- 2 ¼ lbs mixed seafood – mussels, clams, squid, cuttlefish, prawns
- 9 oz diced lean pork
- Optional: a handful diced chorizo or serrano ham

Picada
- 2 tablespoons olive oil
- 2 garlic cloves, peeled and chopped
- 1 tablespoon blanched almonds
- 1 tablespoon chopped parsley
- 1 tablespoon paprika
- 1 teaspoon powdered cinnamon
- ½ teaspoon powdered clove
- 1 lemon, juice and grated zest
- 1 glass dry sherry or white wine
- 12 strands saffron, lightly toasted and soaked in a splash of boiling water
- 1 large onion, finely chopped
- 2–3 large tomatoes, skinned and chopped (or tinned plum tomatoes)

SET THE PASTA, seafood and pork aside while you begin preparing the sauce.

Heat half the oil in a small frying pan. Fry the almonds and garlic till golden, stir in the parsley and let it sizzle and crisp. Tip the contents of the pan into the food processor and process to a paste with the spices, saffron and its soaking water, the lemon juice and zest. Dilute with sherry or wine, and reserve.

To prepare the rest, heat the remaining oil in a large frying pan or raw iron *paellera*, add the pork (and the optional chorizo/ham) and the onion, and fry gently till the meat is cooked through and the onions are soft and golden (15–20 minutes). Push the meat and onions aside and sprinkle in the pasta. Let the pasta sizzle and fry to a rich golden brown. Add the tomatoes and bubble up, then pour in a glass of water. Bubble up again and stir in the almond sauce. Bubble up again, turn down the heat and leave to simmer gently for 5 minutes. Place the seafood on top, bring back to a fierce bubble, turn down the heat and cook till the shellfish have opened, the pasta is perfectly tender and the juices have almost evaporated – another 5 minutes (about 10 minutes in all).

Set the pan in the middle of the table for everyone to help themselves – as with paella, it is traditional to eat the portion immediately in front of you, working neatly from the outside to the middle.

Turkish tomato pilaf with pinenuts

The Turkish pilaf, as with the Spanish paella and Italian risotto, differs from the steamed rice dishes of the Oriental tradition in that the rice is given a preliminary frying with its flavourings. As with the Catalan *fideu* (see left), the dish can be made with rice-shaped pasta in non-rice-growing areas. Turkish pasta, *tarhonya*, as with all other pastas, and with Morocco's couscous, is simply a response to the need to convert perishable seed-foods to a storeable grain-food. If you stick to using rice, it's still nice to include a handful of grain-shaped pasta for a delicate change.

Serves 4–6

HEAT THE OIL in whatever pan you use to make a risotto. As soon as the surface is lightly hazed with blue, add the garlic and matchsticked peppers and fry gently until the vegetables soften – allow about 5 minutes and don't them brown. Add the rice and pasta and turn in the oil until translucent.

Meanwhile, halve the tomatoes horizontally and, holding the curved side in your hand, grate the flesh into a bowl, leaving an empty skin in one hand and a good ladleful of juicy pulp in the bowl. At the same time, bring the stock or water to the boil.

Add the tomato pulp to the rice, bubble up and stir vigorously for a couple of minutes till well mixed and soupy. Add the hot stock or water, bubble up again, reduce the heat and simmer for 15–18 minutes without stirring till the rice is almost tender but still retains a nutty little kernel. Remove the pan from the heat, cover and leave to rest for 10 minutes to allow the rice to finish swelling. The dish should be juicy but not soupy.

Finish with a sprinkle of toasted pine kernels or sesame seeds, and serve with quartered lemons, cos lettuce leaves and Turkish *pide* (or any other pitta-type flatbread) for scooping.

Ingredients
- 10–12 oz risotto rice
- 2 tablespoons Turkish *tarhonya* or any rice-shaped pasta
- 4 tablespoons olive or sesame oil
- 2 garlic cloves, chopped
- 1–2 juicy red peppers, de-seeded and matchsticked
- 2 pints vegetable stock or plain water
- 1 ½ lbs ripe tomatoes
- 1–2 tablespoons toasted pine kernels or sesame seeds

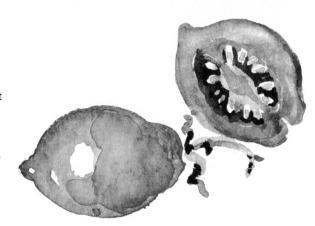

> *Turkish pasta, tarhonya, as with all other pastas (and Morocco's couscous), is simply a response to the need to convert perishable seed-foods to a storeable grain-food*

Carnian polenta with fried cheese

A large copper pot is the traditional cooking implement for the pale ivory-coloured cornmeal from the northeastern Italian region of Carnia. A wood fire is recommended as the heat-source, since the pot, say the Carnians, should be subjected to varying degrees of heat – first high, then low, then high once more.

Serves 4–6

SIFT THE POLENTA to remove any lumps. Bring the water to the boil with the salt. Give it a stir with a wooden spoon to get a whirlpool going, and trickle in the polenta in a steady stream, like making porridge. Keep the heat high until the mixture belches and bubbles. Then turn it down and keep stirring as it thickens. Turn up the heat at the end till the base cracks and smokes.

Between 30–40 minutes (some cook it for an hour) should see it as firm as well-set porridge, ready to be turned out – splat – straight onto the table, peasant-style, or onto a hot serving dish if that's what you prefer. It should come out in the form of a large cake, leaving behind a crisp crust, smoking and singed, which is eaten for breakfast, much like cornflakes.

The traditional way to divide your polenta between participants is to cut it into wedges with a linen thread wound round the handle of a polenta-board, not forgetting to mark the top with the sign of the cross to stop the devil stealing the leftovers.

Serve with *frico*, toasted cheese. For this you will need a pound of hard cheese grated the day

before, tossed to separate the strands and left to dry overnight, and a small frying pan. Heat the pan and sprinkle it with a single layer of grated cheese. Squish the cheese down with a fork as it melts and crisps. When you have a nice brown lacy pancake, flick it out (don't turn it to cook the other side). Repeat until all the cheese has been fried.

Ingredients
- 8–10 oz coarse-ground polenta
- About 1 ½ pints water
- 1 teaspoon salt

The toasted cheese – *frico*
- 1 lb hard cheese (anything hard enough to grate)

Orecchiette with broccoli and anchovies

Orecchiette – the name means 'little ears' – are small pasta shells which look like half-hazelnuts and, when handmade, are shaped on the thumb. The seasoning is fiery little *peperoncini*, the very small, very hot dried chillis which replaced expensive peppercorns as soon as New World vegetables arrived via Venice.

Serves 4

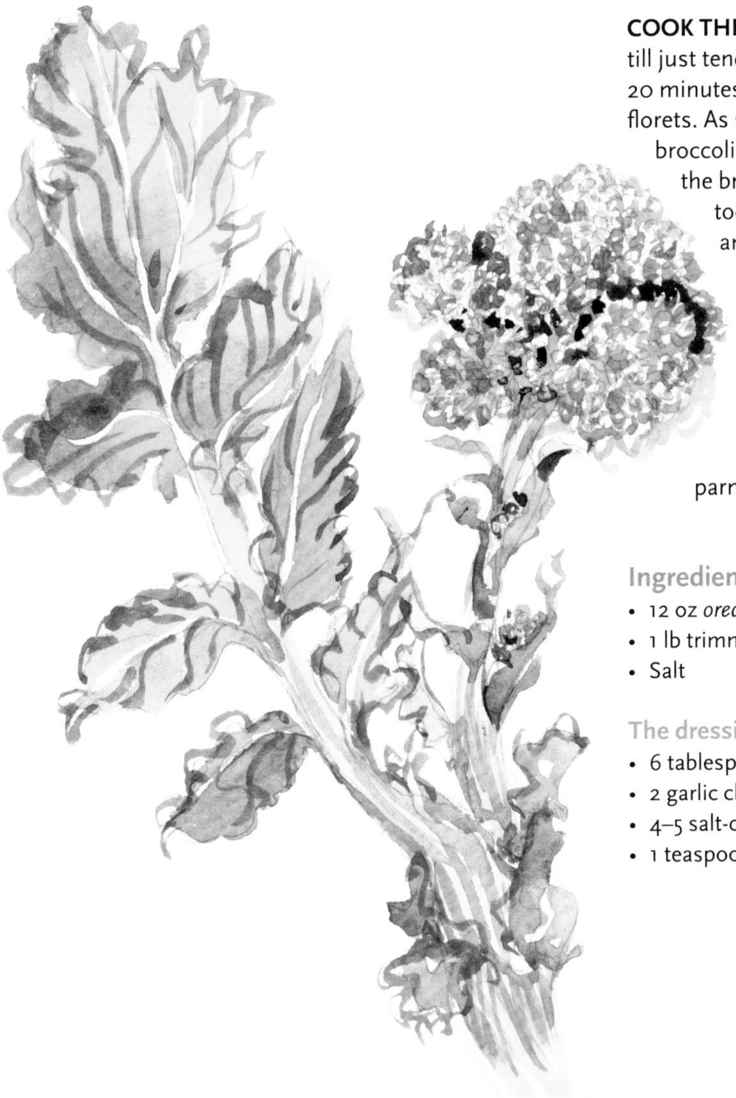

COOK THE PASTA in plenty of boiling salted water till just tender – hard durum wheat pasta takes about 20 minutes. Divide the broccoli into small bite-sized florets. As soon as the pasta is nearly done, add the broccoli, return the pan rapidly to the boil, wait till the broccoli is until tender, then drain, but not too thoroughly. Remove the broccoli spears and chop them roughly.

Meanwhile, prepare the dressing. Warm the oil in a small pan, add the garlic and let it soften for a minute or two, then mash in the broccoli, anchovies and chilli. Dress the pasta with the contents of the pan. No more salt should be necessary.

You can hand-grate pecorino or parmesan on top if you wish.

Ingredients

- 12 oz *orecchiette* or any other small shell-shaped pasta
- 1 lb trimmed broccoli spears
- Salt

The dressing

- 6 tablespoons olive oil
- 2 garlic cloves, slivered
- 4–5 salt-cured anchovies, crushed
- 1 teaspoon flaked dried chilli

Ants climbing trees

A charmingly titled Far Eastern recipe from Lindsey Bareham's *Hungry?* (Penguin, 2008), a collection of well-written, easy-to-follow recipes for students on a budget – hence useful for the rest of us as well. You can make this with minced chicken or sausage meat, says Lindsey. Vegetarians can replace the meat with diced tofu or chopped nuts, and if you can't lay your hands on chilli-bean sauce, a tablespoon of peanut butter and a shake of Tabasco does the trick.

Serves 4

COMBINE THE PORK, light soy sauce, sugar, cornflour and chilli-bean sauce in a bowl and leave for 20 minutes. Pour boiling water over the noodles and leave for 3–4 minutes till tender and transparent.

Finely slice the green part of one spring onion and reserve it for serving. Trim and slice the remaining white and the second spring onion.

Heat the oil in a wok or roomy frying pan and cook the spring onion and the chilli for about 30 seconds. Add the pork mixture and stir-fry for 2–3 minutes, then add the noodles and mix well. Add the chicken stock and dark soy sauce and bubble up. Cook for a few more minutes till the liquid has all but disappeared into the noodles. Finish with the reserved uncooked sliced green spring onion.

Ingredients
- 8 oz minced pork
- 2 tablespoons light soy sauce
- 1 tablespoon sugar
- 1 teaspoon cornflour
- 1 tablespoon chilli-bean sauce
- 10 oz bean thread vermicelli
- 2 spring onions
- 1 small red chilli, de-seeded and finely chopped
- 3 tablespoons peanut oil
- ¼ chicken stock cube dissolved in 4 tablespoons boiling water
- 1 tablespoon dark soy sauce

Ravioles of spiced pork

Try the old way with a free-range porker from *Cooking and Dining in Medieval England* by Peter Brears (Prospect Books, 2008). Mr Brears ranks high among that select band of scholarly reconstruction cooks who can produce an Elizabethan banquet in a flash of a swan's pin-feather.

Serves 4

FIRST MAKE THE dough. Put the flour into a bowl, make a well in the centre and work in just enough cold water with a knife-blade to form a stiff dough. Turn onto a floured board, knead until smooth, roll out to a thickness of approximately one-sixteenth of an inch.

Make the stuffing. Chop and then grind the pork, dates, figs, egg yolk, saffron, cloves, black pepper and sugar to a smooth paste, moistening it with a little of the chicken stock, then stir in the currants.

Roll out the dough, and cut into eight 4-inch rounds. Spread the mixture on 4 of the rounds, leaving the edges clear. Dampen the edges, cover with the remaining rounds and seal the edges, excluding all air.

Bring the remaining stock to the boil in a large pan, put in the ravioles and boil for 10 minutes. Put them into a deep dish with the stock, and sprinkle them with the mixed grated cheese and ginger to finish.

Ingredients
Dough
- 8 oz plain white flour
- About ¼ pint cold water

Stuffing
- 8 oz lean pork
- 4 dates, chopped
- 4 dried figs, chopped
- 1 egg yolk
- 1 ½ pints chicken stock
- Large pinch of saffron
- Pinch ground cloves and black pepper
- 1 teaspoon sugar
- 1 tablespoon currants

To finish
- 2 oz grated cheese
- A pinch powdered ginger

Red wine risotto

A recipe from Nancy Harmon Jenkins's *Essential Mediterranean* (HarperCollins US, 2003). Nancy spends much of her time in the wilder parts of Tuscany and knows practically all there is to know about the cooking of Italy, and I travel with her whenever the opportunity arises. Barolo is the recommended wine, but any robust red wine will do, and arborio is a good choice of rice, though Italian chefs insist on one of the small-grain varieties – carnaroli or vialone nano – because their short, fat grains cook to a more satisfactory creaminess. One American cup is a scant ½ pint: use a standard coffee-mug as a measure.

Serves 4

WARM THE WINE in a pan to just below the simmering point. In another pan, heat the stock. In a third – heavy-duty – saucepan, melt the butter gently with the olive oil, add the onion and cook until soft – don't let it brown.

Add the rice and raise the heat a little. Cook, stirring, till the rice is translucent. Add a ladleful of the warm wine and raise the heat a little more. Cook, stirring, till the wine has been absorbed. Lower the heat a little and add more wine. Continue till all has been absorbed. Don't let the rice dry out completely between additions. Add the stock in the same way till the rice is tender but still a little resistant at the centre – you may not need it all.

Remove from the heat, stir in your choice of truffle preparations along with 2 tablespoons of the grated cheese. Taste and add salt and pepper. Cover and set aside to rest for 5–7 minutes for the rice to finish swelling.

Serve in deep plates, handing round the rest of the cheese separately. Afterwards, and to mop up the sticky bits (no need to change plates), serve a frizzy-leaved winter salad – chicory, escarole – dressed with a handful of salty little capers and this year's olive oil.

Ingredients
- 2 cups red wine (Barolo, if you can get it)
- 2 cups chicken stock
- 1 tablespoon unsalted butter
- 1 tablespoon extra virgin olive oil
- 2 tablespoons finely chopped red onion
- 1 ½ cups risotto rice
- Sea salt and freshly ground pepper
- Optional: 1 tablespoon truffle butter or paste or fragranced oil
- ½ cup grated parmesan

YOUNG VINES BAROLO

Quick cornbread

One of the first dishes Caribbean food guru Rosamund Grant taught her classes in Barbados, to encourage new students. Success, she says, is guaranteed. The baking powder measurement is not a mistake: cornmeal is dense and requires a large amount of raising agent. Serve with any rich, juicy stew.

Serves 6

SIFT ALL THE dry ingredients together. Whisk the milk and eggs to blend, then whisk in the melted butter. Combine the dry and the wet to make a smooth batter. Pour into a 2-lb loaf tin and bake at 190C/375F/Gas5 for 40–50 minutes, till well risen and browned. Serve hot, sliced and lightly buttered. Any leftovers can be cut into fingers and crisped in a little hot oil – good for breakfast as a dip for hot chocolate or milky coffee.

Ingredients
- 8 oz plain flour
- 8 oz fine-ground cornmeal (polenta)
- 10 level teaspoons baking powder
- 1 level teaspoon powdered cinnamon
- ½ teaspoon salt
- 4 tablespoons sugar
- 15 fl oz milk
- 2 medium eggs
- 2 oz butter, melted

Lesley Blanch's emerald pilau

A simple rice and spinach dish suitable for both Sunni and Shi'ite Muslims, says the sometime traveller on the wilder shores of love. The recipe was included in Ms Blanch's cookbook *Around the World in Eighty Dishes*, published shortly after Mrs David reminded her countrywomen that foreign food could taste good. Lesley's recipes, as befits a woman *sui generis* – a description her biographer, Anne Boston, ascribes to Audrey Withers, Ms Blanch's editor at *Vogue* – are as much about people and place as they are about the cooking.

Serves 4–6

COOK THE SPINACH in fast-boiling salted water till tender. Drain, reserving both water and leaves.

Meanwhile, turn the rice in the oil with a knob of butter and fry gently till transparent. Add the spinach water to more than cover the rice, and bubble up. Season, turn down the heat, add more spinach water as needed, and leave to simmer gently till the rice is *al dente* but not sloppy. Stir in the spinach leaves, reheat till steaming, then stir in the nutmeg and plenty more butter.

Ingredients
- 2 lbs spinach, rinsed and chopped
- 3 breakfast cups long-grain rice
- 3 tablespoons grapeseed or vegetable oil
- Butter
- 1 rounded teaspoon freshly grated nutmeg

" A simple rice and spinach dish suitable for both Sunni and Shi'ite Muslims, says the sometime traveller on the wilder shores of love "

Chapter 6
Vegetables

The Department of Uncheckable Information says that 43 per cent of us will be vegetarians within the next decade. Which is an awful lot of people eating nothing but stuff we haven't got the space to grow, having spread concrete over an unreasonably high proportion of our green and pleasant land.

The DUI also says that roughly half of our food-growing farmland – some 2.5 million hectares – will have to be planted with oilseed rape in order to meet five per cent of our future transport needs with biofuel. But since it takes half a ton of fossil fuel to produce a ton of biofuel – well, back to the drawing board.

It's all a bit of a worry. No wonder so many of us are shouldering spades and joining the queue for allotments. For these, however, Uncheckable Info predicts a seven-year wait (the Rumpelstiltskin option). Meanwhile, if none of us ate meat and we all planted cabbages up and down the motorways (the Bulgarian option), world hunger could be solved in a trice. Which would leave us cold-climate carnivores a little shortchanged, it being a verifiable truth that the hotter the climate, the less we need meat.

But if climate change means we'll all soon be basking in sub-Saharan sunshine, we won't need oilseed rape to heat our houses, we won't have to fly to Mediterranean beaches to get a suntan, and we won't mind a bit if we don't eat meat as long as we get our protein in other forms – by which I don't mean sausage-shaped tofu mince or shepherd's pie without the lamb. As a nation of meat-eaters – climate and landscape favours pasture over arable – vegetables are traditionally treated as supporting cast rather than the main event.

Climate and latitude – a short growing season, high rainfall, unreliable levels of sunshine, frost in winter – limit what we can grow for ourselves. We can handle roots, greens and the hardier members of the cabbage family, with pod-vegetables – peas and green beans – available for a short time in the summer. Everything else needs careful cosseting to bring it to maturity – which was all very well for the rich of Queen Victoria's day, who employed armies of gardeners on their country estates to tend exotic vegetables and tropical fruit in heated beds and greenhouses. Ordinary country folk made do with what came up in the kale-yard; town-dwellers had their supplies from the market gardens which once surrounded our cities.

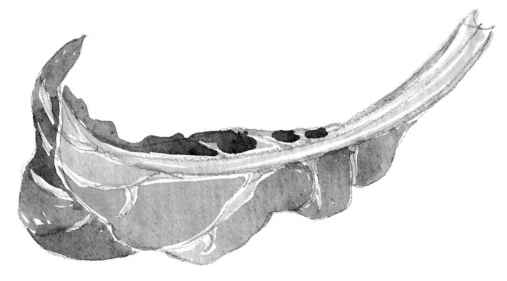

Tian de blea

In Old Nice, one time capital of the independent County of Provence, this thick juicy green egg-cake is known as *la trouchia* and sold, cut in thick wedges, in every cooked-food shop as a mid-morning snack. *Blea* – or chard, a dark-leaved thick-stalked member of the beet family – was so popular in the region that the inhabitants were known as *caga-blea*, 'cack-chard' to put it delicately. Save the stalks to cook like asparagus and serve warm with a mustardy vinaigrette.

Serves 4–6

PACK THE SHREDDED chard into a roomy saucepan with a table-spoon of the olive oil and the garlic cloves crushed with a little salt. Add 2–3 tablespoons of water, lid tightly and cook over a high heat till the leaves wilt, allowing 4–5 minutes.

Transfer to a sieve to drain and cool. Squeeze hard to remove excess moisture.

Meanwhile, gently fry the diced aubergine in 3 tablespoons of the olive oil till perfectly soft – a little salt will help the vegetable yield up its water – and transfer to a sieve set over a bowl to catch the drip-pings. Press to remove excess oil. Return the drippings and add the rest of the oil to the pan.

Fry the pepper strips till soft and lightly caramelised.

Preheat the oven to 150C/ 300F/ Gas3.

Choose a round gratin dish, diameter about 10 inches – so much the better if you have an earthenware *tian* or *cazuela*, the Spanish equivalent. Rub the inside with a cut clove of garlic and trickle with just enough oil to stop the contents sticking.

In a roomy bowl, fork the eggs to blend, season with nutmeg, salt and pepper, stir in the vegetables and cheese, and tip everything into the baking dish, poking the solids down so that all is submerged by egg. If you need another egg, mix it in. Transfer to the oven and bake for 35–40 minutes until the egg is just set but still trembling in the middle – it'll firm up as it cools.

Ingredients
- 1 lb chard leaves (no stalks), rinsed and shredded
- About 6 tablespoons olive oil
- 1–2 garlic cloves
- 1 medium aubergine, diced
- 1 red pepper, de-seeded and cut into strips
- 6 eggs, forked to blend
- 2–3 tablespoons grated cheese (cantal, gruyère, emmental, cheddar)
- ½ teaspoon freshly grated nutmeg
- Salt and pepper

Pain de laitue

Lettuces baked with eggs and cream – basically a vegetarian paté – from the great Richard Olney, the man who introduced America to the fresh-from-the-market home cooking of the French bourgeoisie. If Julia Child taught Jackie Kennedy's generation how to master the art of *haute cuisine*, it was Olney who brought the traditional back to earth.

When *Simple French Food* was first published in the 1970s, Americans already knew that French food was something to which they should aspire, but believed that it needed either impossible-to-obtain ingredients, such as sea-urchins (MFK Fisher), or took many hours of toil and several pages of instruction to master (Mrs Child). But the existence of a Gallic tradition of straightforward home cooking was a new and attractive notion, inspiring new-wave chefs such as Alice Waters at Chez Panisse, Deborah Madison at Greens and home cooks at farmers' markets across the land.

Serves 4

PICK OVER AND wash the lettuce leaves as for a salad, parboil them, counting 3–4 minutes from the time that the water returns to a boil, drain, refresh beneath cold running water, and squeeze them free of excess moisture. Chop them.

Preheat the oven to 350C/180F/Gas4.

Whisk together the cream, eggs and seasonings (taste to check), stir in the lettuce and pour into a buttered charlotte mould or deep baking dish against the bottom of which has been firmly pressed a round of buttered parchment paper (to facilitate the un-moulding). Cook in a bain-marie for 45–50 minutes, till the centre is firm to the touch.

Run a knife round the edges before unmoulding, lift off the round of parchment, and serve it as an accompiment to a roast.

As a course apart, it is attractive with a lightly-buttered tomato sauce. To prepare, simply scald, skin, de-seed and dice ripe tomatoes and stew them gently to a purée with a knob of butter.

Ingredients
- 4 heads loose-leaf (round) lettuces
- ½ pint double cream
- 4 eggs
- Salt, pepper, nutmeg
- Butter for the mould

Courgette gratin

Another of Richard Olney's easy recipes from *Simple French Food* (Grub Street reprint, 2003).
Mr Olney, the man who converted his countrymen to the notion that good food might be possible
for every day, gives several recipes for what are known in the US by their Italian name, *zucchini*
– useful for anyone with a glut in the garden. Here a familiar dish is finished with a *persillade*,
parsley and garlic chopped to a paste, a distinctively French flavouring.

Serves 4

TOSS THE COURGETTE slices, salted, in the olive oil
over a high flame (tossing every few seconds) for 5–6
minutes or until limp and but lightly coloured.

Preheat the oven to 220C/425F/Gas7.

Mix together the remaining ingredients, beating
with a fork, stir in the sautéed courgettes and smooth
the mixture into an oiled gratin dish. Finish with a
sprinkle of oil, and bake for half an hour, till browned
and bubbling.

> *In Simple French Food,*
> *Richard Olney converted his*
> *American countrymen to the*
> *notion that good food might be*
> *possible for every day*

Ingredients
- 1 lb courgettes sliced coin-thin
- 3 tablespoons olive oil
- Salt and pepper
- 2 slices stale bread, crusts removed, soaked in
  hot water, well-squeezed
- 4 oz gruyère cut into dice
- Persillade: 2 garlic cloves pounded to a paste in
  a mortar with a handful of chopped parsley
- 1 egg
- More olive oil for finishing

Yarrow polenta with almond crust

The cooking time of yarrow depends on its maturity, says Vivien Weise in *Cooking Weeds* (Prospect, 2007). Best stick to young spring growth and discard any tough stalks.

Serves 4 as a main course

BRING THE STOCK to the boil and stir in the polenta. Simmer gently for 20–30 minutes (depending on the freshness and fineness of the grind), stirring throughout, till you have a thick, soft porridge.

Meanwhile, fry the onions and garlic in half the butter and season with a little salt, pepper and nutmeg. When the onion is transparent, stir in the chopped yarrow and cook for 5–6 minutes, till tender, and reserve. Sauté the almonds in the remaining butter, and reserve.

In a gratin dish, layer the polenta and the yarrow mixture, finishing with polenta. Top with the almonds and their buttery juices. Bake at 200C/400F/Gas6 for 20–25 minutes.

Ingredients

- 1 ½ pints vegetable stock
- 8 oz polenta
- 2 large onions, finely chopped
- 4 handfuls young yarrow, finely chopped
- 2 garlic cloves, crushed
- 2 oz butter
- Salt, pepper, nutmeg
- 3 oz flaked almonds

Pumpkin garbure with cinnamon and thyme

A garbure, as I'm sure you know, is a sheaf or bundle (call it an armful), and the dish which takes its name is one of that amiable group of anything-goes vegetable stews which are the traditional midday meal of France's rural households. For a more substantial dish, replace the baguette with thickly sliced sourdough or any other robust country bread. Replace the pumpkin with cabbage, or turnip, or parsnips, or anything else which takes your fancy.

Serves 4 as a main dish

PREHEAT THE OVEN to 180C/350F/Gas4.

Heat 2 tablespoons of the oil in a roomy frying pan and fry the onions gently, stirring regularly, till soft and golden. Allow at least 20 minutes, take your time and don't let the onions brown.

Oil the base of a deep gratin dish – whichever one you usually use to serve 4 people. Lay in half the bread slices, spread with half the onion sprinkled with a little thyme, salt and pepper, and top with the sliced pumpkin sprinkled with a little cinnamon, salt and pepper. Cover with another layer of onion, seasoned as before, and pour in the hot stock. Top with the remaining bread slices – they should cover the entire surface, but it doesn't matter if there are gaps. Sprinkle with cheese.

Bake for 40–50 minutes, until the pumpkin is perfectly tender and the top deliciously brown and bubbling. Check after half an hour and cover with foil if necessary.

Ingredients

- 3 tablespoons olive oil
- 2 large onions, finely sliced
- 1 full-size baguette (or sourdough bread), thickly sliced
- 2-lb piece of pumpkin, de-seeded, peeled and sliced
- 1 teaspoon crumbled thyme
- ½ teaspoon powdered cinnamon
- Salt and crushed black pepper
- 2 pints chicken or vegetable stock
- 2–3 tablespoons grated cheese (cantal, gruyère, cheddar)

Swiss mushroom ragout

A mix of wild fungi is better than a single species: a blend of peppery pieds de mouton, bland chanterelles and gluey cèpes gives a good balance of texture and flavour. But if you use cultivated mushrooms – supermarket blends of 'exotics' usually include a fair proportion of oriental cultivars, such as straw mushrooms and shiitake – double the volume of thyme.

Serves 4

CLEAN AND SLICE the fungi. Melt the butter in a casserole and gently fry the garlic, onion and herbs. Stir in the fungi. Season and cook gently until the moisture is steamed out and the fungi start to fry a little. Add the wine, let it bubble up until the alcohol evaporates. Off the heat, stir in the egg yolk lightly whisked with a little of the wine juices – it'll thicken the sauce a little. Don't reboil or it'll scramble. Serve with triangles of white bread fried in butter – very retro.

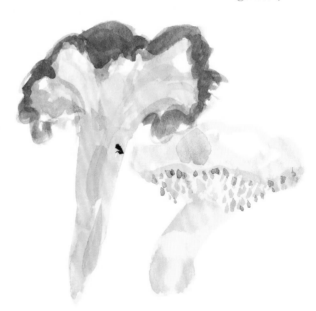

Ingredients
- 1 lb mixed firm-fleshed fungi, wild or cultivated
- 2 oz butter
- 2 garlic cloves, skinned and chopped
- 2 shallots or 1 onion, chopped
- 1 tablespoon chopped parsley
- ½ teaspoon thyme (dried or fresh leaves)
- 1 bay leaf
- 1 glass white wine
- 1 egg yolk

A mix of wild fungi is better than a single species: a blend of peppery pieds de mouton, bland chanterelles and gluey cèpes gives a good balance of texture and flavour

Austrian mushroom goulash

Over fifty years after first publication, Gretel Beer's *Austrian Cooking* is still as good as it gets (André Deutsch last reprinted it in 1998). As befits a nation at the crossroads of Europe, Austrian cooks borrow happily from both east and west – Hungary as well as Germany and France. The result is luxurious as well as generous, matching French elegance to German appetites with a touch of Hungarian exuberance. Hungarians count five varieties of paprika, each with its own distinctive colour and flavour, from fierce and fiery to mild and sweet.

Serves 4

MELT THE BUTTER in a saucepan and gently fry the chopped onion. Add the mushrooms, stir, and add paprika, salt and pepper. Lid and simmer gently until the mushrooms have yielded up their liquid and begin to sizzle a little (don't let the mix begin to brown or the paprika will acquire a bitter flavour).

Sprinkle with flour, stir to blend, and add the beef broth. Cook gently for a few minutes till the juices begin to thicken, and then stir in the soured cream. Bubble up till well blended.

Serve with buttered noodles, or white rice, or bread dumplings (Austrians do love a dumpling – for *kirschknödel*, see page 136).

Shake those lederhosen – it's thigh-slapping good.

Ingredients
- 2 oz butter
- 1 small onion, finely chopped
- 1 lb mixed wild and cultivated mushrooms, cleaned and sliced
- 1 heaped tablespoon mild sweet paprika (more if you like)
- A ladleful of beef broth
- 1 scant tablespoon plain flour
- ½ pint soured cream
- Salt and pepper

Himmel und Erde

Himmel und Erde, 'heaven and earth', a combination of earthly potatoes and heavenly apples, makes a substantial winter main course in the German tradition. Serve it on its own, or with a juicy pork chop or a succulent pair of bratwurst, Germany's all-meat grilling sausage. German housewives would never tolerate the rusk-bulked British banger, and Eliza Acton agrees: her sausage recipe is pure pork in proportions of 3 lbs lean to 2 lbs fat. No rusk. Ever. Explain this to your butcher and persuade him to make up a batch. You never know, it might catch on.

Serves 4

SKIN THE COOKED potatoes while still warm and cut into chunks of a similar size to the apple quarters.

Melt the butter in a heavy frying pan. As soon as it sizzles, add the apples and potatoes, turning them carefully until they brown a little. Season with salt, pepper and nutmeg or allspice. Serve with or without meat – or maybe a fried egg.

You might also consider the inclusion of a handful of diced streaky to fry in the butter with the apples and potatoes, though unless you have a source which cures its own pig-meat and produces firm dry streaky with enough fat to fry crisp, choose German speck or Italian pancetta.

Ingredients

- 2 lbs mature potatoes, scrubbed and boiled in their jackets
- 2 lbs eating apples, peeled, cored and quartered
- 2 oz unsalted butter
- ½ teaspoon ground nutmeg or allspice
- Salt and pepper

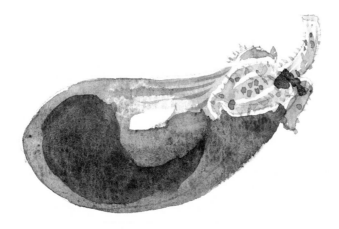

Parmigiana di melanzane

A speciality of Puglia and not, as might be supposed, anything to do with parmesan cheese, this is an oven-baked layering of aubergines and tomatoes, meatless but otherwise much like the Greek moussaka. Puglia is a region known for the excellence of its vegetables, an abundance of oil from ancient olive groves, preserved fish, bread and pasta made with hard durum wheat, fresh and matured cheeses, and an ingenious way with a limited store cupboard. Allied to this is a strong historical connection with both sides of the eastern Mediterranean, both Arab and Greek.

Serves 4

HEAT THE OIL gently in a roomy frying pan. Slip in the aubergine slices – as many as will fit in a single layer – and fry them till they soften, brown a little and begin to yield up their oil. Transfer to a colander set over a bowl to catch the drippings. Continue till all are done.

Meanwhile, make a thick tomato sauce. Put the tomatoes, garlic, thyme, sugar and chilli flakes in a liquidiser and whizz to a purée. Transfer the purée to a small pan, add the drippings from the bowl, season and heat. Leave to bubble and thicken while you finish frying the aubergines.

Layer the aubergines with the tomato sauce and mozzarella in a gratin dish, finishing with mozzarella. Trickle with the last drainings of the oil. Bake at 180C/350F/Gas4 for 25–30 minutes till brown and bubbling.

Ingredients

- 2–3 fine fat aubergines, sliced as thick as a pound coin
- About 6 tablespoons extra virgin olive oil
- 2–3 garlic cloves, crushed with salt
- 1 large tin or 2 lbs fresh plum tomatoes, scalded, skinned and chopped
- 1 teaspoon thyme leaves
- A little sugar
- ½ teaspoon chilli flakes
- Salt (no pepper)
- 2–3 fresh mozzarella cheeses, thinly sliced

Asparagus gratin

By the colour of your asparagus shall you be known, say those who traditionally supply the markets of the north with early vegetables from the south. The Germans demand fat stalks of a creamy white, the French like theirs just tinged with purple, the British prefer perfectly green from tip to toe. The precise tint of the morning crop – asparagus appears like magic overnight – depends on the amount of time the shoots are exposed to sunlight – a matter of hours. To fetch the highest price, the spears must be straight and of identical length and diameter – which, inevitably, leads to plenty of wastage. This is how the asparagus growers of Haute Provence like to eat their unsellable spears.

Serves 4 as a light lunch

WASH THE ASPARAGUS carefully (their beds are sandy) and snap off the tender tips, saving the stalks for soup.

Cook the tips until just tender in boiling salted water: allow 5–6 minutes – don't let them boil fiercely or they'll break. Drain thoroughly and arrange in a gratin dish.

Meanwhile, melt the butter in a heavy saucepan, stir in the flour and fry till sandy, but don't let it brown. Whisk in the broth gradually (if you're not sure of your blending skills, heat the broth first), and simmer gently till the sauce thickens. Stir in the garlic, parsley, ham, eggs and cream cheese, and remove from the heat. Taste and season with a little nutmeg, salt and pepper.

Pour the sauce over the asparagus and sprinkle with grated cheese. Slip the dish under the grill for 10–15 minutes till brown and bubbling.

Ingredients

- About 2 lbs white, green or purple-tipped asparagus (broken spears are fine)
- 2 tablespoons butter or oil
- 2 tablespoons flour
- 1 pint chicken broth or milk
- 2 garlic cloves, finely chopped
- 2 heaped tablespoons chopped parsley
- 2–3 tablespoons finely chopped ham or lean bacon
- 2–3 hard-boiled eggs, finely chopped
- About 4 tablespoons cream cheese or mascarpone
- ½ teaspoon grated nutmeg
- Salt and pepper

To finish

- Grated hard cheese (cantal, gruyère, cheddar)

By the colour of your asparagus shall you be known. The Germans demand fat stalks of a creamy white, the French like theirs tinged with purple, the British prefer green

Pommes boulangères

Rib-sticking cabbage and tatties as they like it in northern France, from chef Jean-Christophe Novelli's mum. Mr Novelli has been described in the *New York Times* as the world's sexiest chef. And he gives great recipe, too.

Serves 4

PREHEAT THE OVEN to 190C/375F/Gas5.

Slice the potatoes very thinly. Drop the cabbage leaves into boiling salted water for 1 minute, remove and drain. Melt the butter with the olive oil in a frying pan and fry the onions, garlic, thyme and bay leaves gently for 2–3 minutes, till the onion has softened.

Butter a gratin dish and layer in the potatoes, onions and cabbage, finishing with a layer of potato. Pour in enough hot stock to cover everything. Season.

Bake for about 45 minutes uncovered to allow the stock to evaporate (but don't let it dry out). Ten minutes before the end, cover the top with the slivered cheese. Continue to bake till golden and bubbling and the potatoes are cooked right through.

Ingredients

- 5–6 Savoy cabbage leaves
- 1 lb floury potatoes
- 1 oz butter
- 2 tablespoons olive oil
- 2 large onions, sliced
- 3 garlic cloves, chopped
- 4 thyme sprigs, de-stalked and chopped
- 2 bay leaves
- About 2 pints hot strong chicken or vegetable stock
- Salt and freshly ground pepper
- 6 oz strong cheese (Red Leicester for choice), slivered

> *Rib-sticking cabbage and tatties as they like it in northern France, from chef Jean-Christophe Novelli's mum. Mr Novelli has been described as the world's sexiest chef*

Valencian vegetable casserole

Spain, no question, is no longer a culinary backwater. Spanish chefs, everyone knows, are the hottest thing to hit the restaurant circuit since Escoffier first told his followers to keep it simple. At Casa Benigna, a small restaurant with a big reputation tucked away in a back alley in Madrid, Valencian granny Carmen Garcia provides the simplicity to her son Norberto's expertise. A chef's value lies in innovation and presentation, the elements which earn the stars and convince the punters the plate is worth the price. Carmen's value, as shown in this everyday dish she has prepared since long before Norberto was born, lies in knowing how to make good ingredients taste exactly as they should.

Serves 3–4 as a main course

TO PREPARE THE artichoke hearts, slice off the hard top of the leaves to expose the cluster of pale spiky little fronds which enclose the choke. Trim the outer leaves right down to the tender bases, then nick out the hairy choke, leaving only the heart. Drop the hearts immediately into a bowl of cold water with a squeeze of lemon – the acid keeps the cut flesh pale.

Gently heat the oil in a roomy frying pan and fry the potato till perfectly soft and lightly browned – don't let the oil overheat. Remove the potato with a draining spoon and transfer to a casserole. Pour out half the oil and reserve.

Meanwhile, cut the artichoke hearts into cubes roughly the same size as the broad beans. Reheat the remaining oil in the frying pan and add the artichoke and beans. Cook gently till all the water has evaporated and tiny bubbles have formed around the vegetable pieces – too high a heat will harden the bean skins. Then transfer the vegetables to the casserole.

Reheat the remaining oil and fry the chopped onion – still gently – till soft and golden. Add the diced ham and let it feel the heat. Transfer the contents of the frying pan to the casserole, add just enough water to cover, and add salt sparingly – the ham is already salty. Bubble up till almost all the

liquid has evaporated, leaving the vegetables bathed in a fragrant, oily little sauce.

Finish with quartered hard-boiled eggs and serve warm rather than piping hot, with a young red wine – a little acidity cuts the richness of the juices – and chunks of bread for mopping. Sliced oranges dressed with honey and toasted slivered almonds would provide an appropriately Valencian conclusion.

Ingredients
- 4–8 young artichokes (depending on size), hearts only
- ½ lemon
- 1 ½ lbs shelled broad beans (frozen is fine)
- About ¼ pint olive oil
- 1 medium potato, peeled and diced
- 1 large onion, finely chopped
- 2 tablespoons diced raw ham (serrano or parma or lean bacon)
- Salt (no pepper)

To finish
- Hard-boiled eggs, quartered

Tuscan winter minestrone

A well-made minestrone is a meal in itself. Fragrant with herbs, rich with olive oil, it should be so thick with vegetables a wooden spoon can stand up in it. All the vegetable chunks should be about the same size in order to cook evenly – one-inch cubes, a baby's mouthful, is about right.

Serves 4 as a main dish

WARM THE OIL in a large stewpot, but don't let it heat to smoking point. Add the leeks and chopped pancetta, and fry for a minute or two.

Add the celery, carrot, parsnip and turnip and toss over the heat for 5 minutes or so. Let them gild a little, but don't let them brown.

Add the water, bay leaves and thyme, season, bring to the boil, turn down the heat and simmer for 10 minutes. Add the potatoes. Bring back to the boil, turn down the heat, lid loosely and simmer for another 15 minutes, until the potatoes are nearly tender. Add the pasta. Bring back to the boil and simmer for another 10 minutes – longer if needed – till both vegetables and pasta are perfectly soft. If necessary, add a little more boiling water – sparingly, since the soup should be good and thick. Stir in the finishing ingredients, bring back to the boil and remove from the heat. Taste and adjust the seasoning.

Serve ladled into deep plates, handing round the cheese with a grater separately.

Ingredients
- 2 tablespoons olive oil
- 2 well-grown leeks, white and green, rinsed, sliced into fine rings
- 2 tablespoons chopped pancetta or lean bacon
- 2 sticks celery, chunked
- 2 well-grown carrots, scraped and chunked
- 1 large parsnip, peeled and chunked
- 2 small turnips, peeled and chunked
- 1–2 bay leaves
- 1 small sprig thyme
- 2 medium potatoes, peeled and chunked
- 2 ½ pints boiling water
- 2 oz macaroni or any medium-sized dried pasta
- Salt and pepper

To finish
- Chopped parsley
- Finely grated lemon zest
- 1 garlic clove, finely chopped
- Olive oil

To serve
- Parmesan or pecorino for grating

Lebanese green beans in tomato sauce

The glamorous Anissa Helou – loft-dweller in London's fashionable Hoxton, author of *Lebanese Cuisine* (Grub Street, 2008) and leader of fabulous tours to the ancient cities of the wilder shores – says this is the first dish she ever taught herself to cook. As a teenager in Beirut, she and her sisters would sneak down to the family kitchen to cook themselves a midnight feast with whatever they could scrounge. The sauce should be very thick and rich – what else?

Serves 4, with bread

CUT THE BEANS into 2-inch lengths – about as long as your thumb. Rinse under cold water and set aside. If using fresh tomatoes, cover them with boiling water to loosen the skins before you peel and chop.

Put the olive oil, chopped onion and whole unpeeled garlic cloves in a large saucepan that will also accommodate the beans. You can use less garlic if you like, or discard the cloves before serving.

Place the saucepan over a medium heat and fry until the onion turns golden. Add the beans, sprinkle generously with salt, and stir over the heat till they become glossy and turn bright green. Add the chopped tomatoes, mix well, cover the pan, and leave to bubble gently for about 40 minutes, till the sauce is thick and the beans are tender.

Serve at room temperature with hot pitta for scooping.

To eat the village way, says Anissa, tear the pitta bread open and place one half, rough side up, as a plate. Tear the other half into small pieces and use it to scoop up the beans and sauce.

Accompany each mouthful with a squeeze of the cooked garlic clove and a bite of raw spring onion. When you've finished the beans, eat the tomato-soaked bread rolled round a length of onion. For the next 24 hours, steer clear of non-villagers as no one will want to be anywhere near you.

Ingredients
- 1 lb green beans, topped and tailed
- 1 lb tinned plum or fresh ripe tomatoes, peeled and chopped
- 4 tablespoons extra virgin olive oil
- 1 medium onion, finely chopped
- 8 garlic cloves (yes indeed)
- Salt to taste

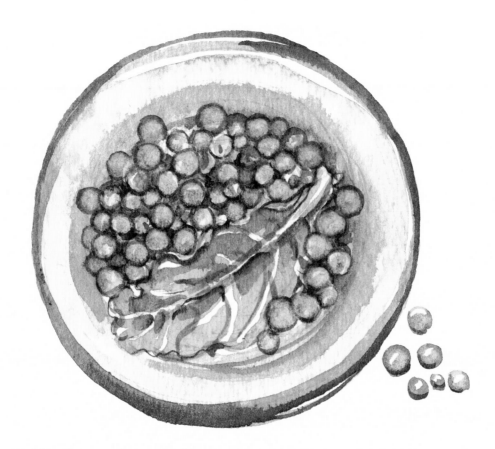

Old peas with cider and bacon

If your freshly gathered peas seem somewhat bullet-like, no matter. Writing just before World War Two, Edward Bunyard – wit, horticulturalist, pomologist (apple-fancier, lest your Latin be a little rusty) – finds much to love in older peas when cooked, as here, gently in well-flavoured juices. 'Who does not prefer women of the world, a little hardened by adversity, to callow youth or crabbed old age?' Indeed. My feelings precisely.

Serves 4–6

PUT ALL THE ingredients (except the butter) in a heavy-based pan, bring to the boil and bubble up for a moment to evaporate the alcohol. Lid and simmer gently for 30–40 minutes till the peas have lost their fresh green colour and the cooking juices are reduced to a couple of tablespoonfuls. Taste, season and stir in the butter to finish.

Ingredients
- 1 ½ lbs shelled elderly peas
- ½ medium onion, diced
- 2–3 lettuce leaves (outer)
- 1 tablespoon diced lean bacon
- ¼ pint dry cider
- 1 level tablespoon sugar
- Salt and freshly milled pepper
- 1 walnut-sized knob unsalted butter

Zwiebelkuchen

A marvellously creamy, yeasty German onion tart much like a superior pizza, perfect for a cold winter in the Black Forest. No need to tell you that veggies can leave out the bacon. This is a rich dough and needs lots of yeast.

Serves 4–6

ALL THE DOUGH ingredients should be warm – put them out in the kitchen well ahead of time. Mix the yeast with the sugar to liquidise it, and then stir in some of the milk-and-water. Sift the flour with the salt and marjoram. Put all the dough ingredients in the food processor and knead everything with the dough-hook into a very wet dough. Or make it by hand in the usual way.

Leave the dough in the bowl, cover it with a clean cloth and put it in a warm place for 20 minutes for the yeast to get working – the high proportion of yeast to flour allows it to work quickly.

Meanwhile, fry the bacon in a little butter till the fat runs, and add the onions to the bacon fat until they soften – but on no account let them brown.

Preheat the oven to 225C/425F/Gas7.

Butter a large baking sheet or your roomiest roasting tin. Pat the dough out flat with a well-floured hand till it's the thickness of your little finger, as if making a pizza base. Top with a juicy layer of onions and bacon.

Make a savoury custard by forking up the eggs with their own volume of soured cream, season with nutmeg, salt and pepper, and trickle over the onions – the rings catch the liquid and it just sort of soaks in.

Bake for 20–25 minutes on the middle rack of the oven, until fragrant and exquisitely gilded. Cut into squares and serve with a curly endive and apple salad dressed with a mustardy vinaigrette.

Ingredients
Dough
- 1 lb strong bread flour
- 2 oz fresh yeast
- 1 level teaspoon sugar
- ½ pint milk-and-water
- 2 level teaspoons salt
- 1 teaspoon dried marjoram
- 4 oz pork lard or butter

Topping
- 2 lbs onions, finely sliced into rings
- 2 tablespoons diced speck (pancetta or streaky bacon will do)
- 2 medium eggs
- ¼ pint soured cream
- 1 teaspoon grated nutmeg
- Salt and pepper

Candied sweet potato mash

The natural sweetness and robust earthiness of the caramelised tuber is good with any spicy West Indian fish or vegetable dish. And it's exotic enough to transform a plain grilled chicken, says Barbados-born Rosamund Grant in *Caribbean and African Cookery* (Grub Street, 2003). Perfect after a day on the beach.

Serves 4, generously

PEEL AND THICKLY slice the sweet potatoes. Place in a saucepan of boiling water (to prevent the vegetable discolouring, add a tablespoonful of oil). Boil for 5 minutes, then drain and reserve.

Preheat the oven to 190C/375F/Gas5. Bring the milk to the boil with the butter. Meanwhile, arrange the sweet potato slices in a buttered gratin dish. Pour in the boiling milk mixture and scatter with the sugar, salt and nutmeg. Cover loosely with foil shiny side down, and bake for 25–30 minutes (remove the foil after the first 15 minutes), till the potatoes are perfectly tender and the top is brown and bubbling.

Ingredients
- 3 lbs sweet potatoes
- ¾ pint full-cream milk
- 2 oz butter
- 1 heaped tablespoon brown sugar
- Pinch of salt
- A little grated nutmeg

Stuffed cabbage leaves

A combination of eco-friendly home-grown cabbage and non-ecologically sound imported rice and raisins, this is nevertheless a cheap and cheerful dish for those who don't want to eat meat. Carnivores, on the other hand, might like to replace the nuts with a little diced ham.

Serves 4–6

SEPARATE OUT THE cabbage leaves, discarding the tough outer leaves. Choose a dozen middle-sized leaves and nick out the base of the central stalk, then scald in boiling water so they're ready to roll. Shred the remaining cabbage heart.

Fry the onions in 2 tablespoons of oil till soft. Add the shredded cabbage and rice and fry for a minute or two, stirring till the grains are transparent. Add the nuts, raisins, and enough water to cover. Season with salt and plenty of pepper. Leave to bubble gently, loosely covered, till the rice has absorbed all the water.

Lay out the leaves, shiny side down. Drop a tea-spoonful of the rice at the stalk end, fold up the sides to enclose the filling, and roll the leaf up like a little bolster. Continue till all are ready and arrange them in a single layer in a gratin dish or shallow saucepan. Trickle with the rest of the oil, lemon juice, and a glass of water. Lid or cover with foil and cook gently for an hour on the hob, or in the oven at 150C /300F/Gas2.

Ingredients
- 1 Savoy cabbage
- 1 medium onion, very finely chopped
- ¼ pint olive oil
- 8 oz round rice
- 2 tablespoons toasted pinenuts or roughly chopped almonds
- 2 tablespoons raisins
- Salt and pepper

To finish
- Juice of 2 lemons

Épinards en surprise

One of the few quick and easy recipes in the great Julia Child's benchmark oeuvre, *Mastering the Art of French Cooking* (Penguin reprint, 2009). Well, you do have to go somewhere else in the book to find out how to make a giant French pancake. The surprise is in the presentation, since the pancake perfectly hides the spinach. For a more substantial dish, says Mrs Child, stir the creamed spinach with a generous handful of sautéed diced ham or mushrooms.

Serves 4

JUST BEFORE SERVING, stir the cheese into the hot braised spinach and heap it in a serving dish. Then cover it with the pancake.

Ingredients

- 2 oz grated Swiss cheese
- 1 ½ lbs spinach braised in stock or cream
- A hot, lightly buttered serving dish about 8 inches in diameter
- A French pancake large enough to cover the spinach completely

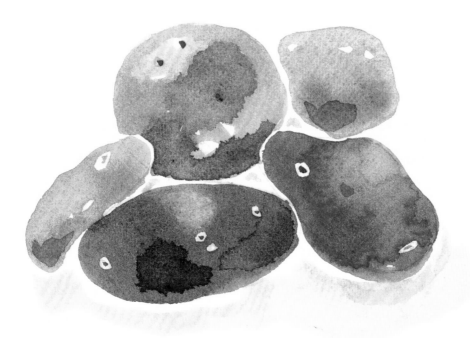

Swiss rösti

The best way ever invented to cook main-crop potatoes. The only thing you need to remember is to cook the potatoes the night before. More classic recipes are to be found in Lyndsay and Patrick Mikanowski's chronicle of the mighty tuber, *Potato* (Grub Street, 2005). She's an ethnologist turned landscape architect, he used to be artistic director at Christian Dior – and, yes, they live just south of Paris, are fabulously well-connected, and their oeuvre is the classiest thing since the Fabergé egg.

Enough for 2 townies or 1 Swiss farmer

THE DAY BEFORE, boil the potatoes in their skins, but leave them slightly underdone – allow 15 minutes (if medium-sized) rather than the full 20. This pre-cooking is essential to allow the starch to re-harden overnight.

Next day, skin the potatoes (or not, as you please) and grate them through the grater's largest holes.

Melt the butter in a roomy frying pan and spread in the grated potatoes. Sprinkle with salt and pepper. Cook over a medium heat for 10 minutes till the potato has softened, stirring to blend in the crispy bits from underneath. Now pat the potato out into a large pancake, stop stirring and let the base fry to a golden crust. Turn it carefully (sliding it out onto a plate first if you're feeling nervous) and fry the other side.

Serve with a fried egg for breakfast. Or for supper with sausages, bacon, fried apples, an endive salad and a glass of fruity Gewürztraminer.

Ingredients
- 2 lbs mature potatoes
- 4 oz butter
- Salt and pepper

Chapter 7
Quick & Easy

Clever people cook. Really they do. Hot news from the evolutionary coal-face is that the application of heat to dinner is what made the difference between big-brained folk like us and teeny-brained folk

This chapter is for those who think they can't cook. Let me put that another way. This chapter is included at the special request of *The Oldie*'s much-respected editor, Richard Ingrams, a man one might think more than capable of applying the hot poker to something which might benefit from a singed buttock.

As the Duke of Devonshire apparently so fetchingly put it on finding out that he had to give up his Italian pastry chef, 'What? Can't a fellow have a biscuit?' Not nowadays he can't. Not unless he cooks it himself. Blame the feminists. Please do. I happen to be one myself – aren't we all? Cooking is for real men, so shape up there at the back. Jamie does it and so does Heston and Hugh. 'Can't cook, won't cook' doesn't cut the mustard any more.

Clever people cook. Really they do. Hot news from the evolutionary coal-face is that the application of heat to dinner is what made the difference between big-brained folk like us (you, me and the editor) and teeny-brained folk (tree-shrews and so forth, the sort we are more than happy to pop in the pot if we're hungry). The problem with raw food, scientists say, is assimilation of nutrients. In short, cooked food is easier to digest than raw, and the brain needs as much nourishment as it can get. If you want to get ahead, boil an egg.

So now you know. Here's how.

In memoriam the glory days, here's a breakfast-cum-dessert recipe from the Windsor Court Hotel in New Orleans

New Orleans granola

In memoriam the glory days, here's a breakfast-cum-dessert recipe from the Windsor Court Hotel, New Orleans's classiest watering hole. Serve it for supper with cream.

Makes about 3 lbs

PREHEAT THE OVEN to 170C/325F/Gas3.

Melt the butter with honey and sugar in a heavy saucepan over a low heat, stirring until all the sugar crystals have dissolved completely. Meanwhile, combine all the dry ingredients together in a roomy bowl.

Stir the butter-honey mixture into the dry ingredients, tossing to blend thoroughly. Transfer to a roasting pan and bake, stirring occasionally to prevent sticking, for about 25 minutes till golden. Don't overcook it: it'll crisp as it cools. Allow to cool completely before storing in an airtight tin.

Ingredients
- 4 oz unsalted butter
- 6 oz honey
- 4 oz brown sugar
- 1 lb rolled oats
- 8 oz shelled unsalted sunflower seeds
- 8 oz slivered almonds
- 6 oz grated coconut
- 6 oz shelled pumpkin seeds
- 4 oz shelled pistachios
- 2 oz pine kernels

Lebanese fattoush

A Lebanese salad, perfect for hot weather. If those who share your table are unused to the notion of a bread salad, set out all the ingredients separately, and encourage everyone to choose their own combinations. Vary the recipe as you please – bread, mint and parsley are the only essentials.

Serves 4–6 as a starter

TOAST OR GRILL the pittas till crisp, then tear or chop into small pieces. Combine with the salad ingredients in a bowl.

Crush the garlic with the salt, and fork in the remaining dressing ingredients. Toss the salad with the dressing, leave to soften and let the flavours marry for 10 minutes or so.

Ingredients

- 4–6 pitta breads
  (or Lebanese *khoubiz*)
- 1 large handful mint,
  leaves only, chopped
- 1 large handful flat-leaf
  parsley, chopped
- 1 small bunch spring onions,
  trimmed and chopped
- 1 small crisp lettuce,
  coarsely shredded
- 1 large handful soft salad leaves
  (purslane, corn salad, baby spinach)
- 1 green pepper,
  de-seeded and diced
- 1 small cucumber, diced
  (peeled or not, as you please)

To dress

- 1–2 garlic cloves
- 1 teaspoon sea salt
- 2–3 lemons, juice and finely
  grated zest
- ¼ pint olive oil

Cheese fondue with new potatoes

The full fondue paraphernalia is not essential if you can't remember where you last saw the set you saved from the Sixties. Do as they do in the Alps: prepare the melted cheese in advance and pour it over the potatoes when your guests take their places at table. Takes you back, doesn't it?

Serves 4

COOK THE POTATOES, scrubbed but unskinned, in plenty of boiling salted water. Drain and fold in a napkin to keep them dry and hot.

Cut the garlic clove in half and rub it round the *caclon*, the fondue pot. Put in both kinds of grated cheese, add the wine and heat very gently, stirring until the cheese melts. Mix in the cornflour to stabilise the buttery juices and the wine. Then stir in the kirsch, if you choose to include it. Add a little more slaked cornflour if the mixture separates.

Call everyone to table and give each person a glass of the same wine which went into the fondue.

Keep the fondue simmering over the spirit-lamp on the table while everyone dips in their potatoes. At the end there will be a crisp brown lace stuck to the bottom of the pan. This is the *dentelle*, the cook's perk. Lift it off and eat it.

Ingredients
- About 2 lbs new potatoes, scrubbed

The fondue
- 1 garlic clove
- 8 oz gruyère, finely chopped or coarsely grated
- 8 oz emmental, finely chopped or coarsely grated
- ½ bottle dry white wine
- 1 teaspoon cornflour or potato starch slaked in a little water
- Optional: a splash of kirsch

Angels and devils on horseback

The battle of good and evil in edible form: what could be more appropriate for the turning year? Oysters are about as sustainable as seafood gets: shove 'em out in a net in a clean loch and they feed themselves.

Serves 2 (6 oysters each is the minimum)

WRAP EACH OYSTER in half a rasher, securing it in place with a toothpick. The molluscs can be raw or lightly poached (3–4 minutes in water with a little white wine, flavoured with thyme and bay leaf).

Stone the prunes (or not, if you're feeling wicked), and wrap each in its half-rasher, securing with a toothpick as before.

Arrange both angels and devils on a baking sheet. Grill fiercely for 2–3 minutes, till the bacon sizzles and begins to brown. Turn all carefully and grill the other side. Season the angels with a squeeze of lemon and the devils with a pinch of cayenne pepper.

> *The battle of good and evil in edible form: what could be more appropriate for the turning year?*

Ingredients
Angels
- 12 oysters, opened
- 6 fine-cut rashers smoked streaky bacon, pancetta or speck
- 1 lemon

Devils
- 12 prunes (ready-to-eat, or plumped up in hot tea)
- 6 fine-cut rashers smoked streaky bacon, pancetta or speck
- Cayenne pepper

English rarebit

This is the definitive Anglo-rarebit as published in 1747 in Hannah Glasse's *The Art of Cookery Made Plain and Easy*. Note the soaking of the bread in claret, the Englishman's favourite tipple.

Serves 1

'TOAST A SLICE of brown bread on both sides, then lay it in a place before the fire, pour a glass of red wine over it, and let it soak the wine up; then cut some cheese very thin, and lay it very thick over the bread, and put in a tin oven before the fire [slip it under the grill], and it will be toasted and browned presently. Serve it away hot.'

Ingredients
- 1 thickish slice brown bread
- 2 oz mature Cheddar cheese, finely slivered
- 2 tablespoons red wine

Scots rarebit

Mistress Margaret Dods, the fictional landlady of the Cleikum Inn in Sir Walter Scott's *St Ronan's Well*, was the pseudonym of the Edinburgh publisher's wife Mrs Christian Isobel Johnstone, a friend of the novelist: her *Cook and Housewife's Manual*, published in Edinburgh in 1826, was much quoted by F Marian McNeill in *The Scots Kitchen* in 1929 – where this recipe comes from.

Serves 1

'**PARE THE CRUST** off a slice of bread cut smooth, and of about a half-inch in thickness. Toast it, but do not let it wither or harden in the toasting.

'Butter it. Grate down mellow Stilton, Gouda, Cheshire, or good Dunlop cheese; and, if not fat, put to it some bits of fresh butter. Put this into a cheese-toaster which has a hot-water reservoir [a heavy pan over a gentle heat is an alternative] and add to it a glassful of well-flavoured brown stout porter, a large teaspoonful of made-mustard, and pepper (very finely ground) to taste.

'Stir the mixture till it is completely dissolved, brown it, and then, filling the reservoir with boiling water, serve the cheese with hot dry or buttered toasts on a separate dish.'

Ingredients
- 2 oz cheese
- 1 very thick slice bread, crusts off
- Butter
- 2 tablespoons stout
- ½ teaspoon English mustard
- Ground pepper

> *Margaret Dods, the fictional landlady of the Cleikum Inn in Sir Walter Scott's St Ronan's Well, was the pseudonym of Christian Isobel Johnstone, whose 'Cook and Housewife's Manual' was published in Edinburgh in 1826*

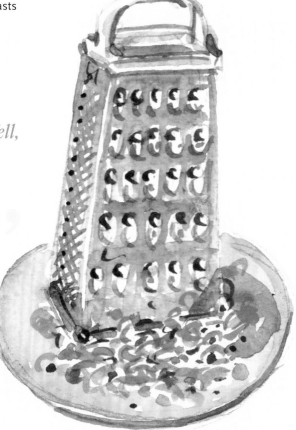

Welsh rarebit

Welsh rarebit is the perfect comfort food for a rainy day in the Cambrian Mountains (where I sketched the farmhouse above). This is the definitive recipe for the Welsh national dish, as given in Lady Llanover's *The First Principles of Good Cookery* first published in 1867, the Welsh equivalent of *Mrs Beeton's Book of Household Management*. Lady L, an Englishwoman born and bred till she married into the aristocracy of South Wales, set about improving the morals and drinking habits as well as the culinary skills of her adopted land. 'Welsh toasted cheese and the melted cheese of England,' she explained, 'are as different in the mode of preparation as the cheese itself; the one being only adapted to strong digestions, and the other being so easily digested.' I have extracted the ingredients in the form of a shopping list, but left the method in Lady L's own words.

Serves 1

'**CUT A SLICE** of the real Welsh cheese, made of sheep and cow's milk; toast it at the fire on both sides, but not so much as to drop; toast a piece of bread less than a quarter inch thick, to be quite crisp, and spread it very thinly with fresh cold butter on one side (it must not be saturated with butter), then lay the toasted cheese on the bread, and serve immediately on a very hot plate.

'The butter on the toast can of course be omitted if not liked, and it is more frequently eaten without butter.'

Ingredients
• 2 oz Welsh cheese (Caerphilly would be correct)
• 1 medium-thick slice of sturdy country bread
• Optional: salty Welsh butter

Mrs Beeton's croûtes au fromage

My own Edwardian edition of young Isabella Beeton's great achievement – first published in book form in 1861 and in many expanded editions thereafter – gives this recipe for toasted cheese under a fashionably French name. The amount of cheese allotted per portion doubles the allowance suggested by other writers.

Serves 1

'**SLICE THE CHEESE** very thinly. Knead the butter, mustard and a good pinch of cayenne well together on a plate. Prepare 1 slice of buttered toast, trim the edges, cover with half the cheese slices, and spread on half the butter.

'Now add the remainder of the slices of cheese, cover with butter as above, and cook in a Dutch oven before the fire [or slip under a hot grill] until the cheese is melted. Serve as hot as possible.'

Ingredients
- 4 oz Cheshire or Cheddar cheese
- 1 oz butter
- 1 mustard-spoonful of dry mustard
- Pinch cayenne pepper
- Buttered toast

Migas with chorizo

Breadcrumbs, *migas*, crisped in olive oil with a flavouring of garlic and *pimentón*, is how they like to eat up the last of the week's bread in Castile, Spain's high central plateau. The chorizo is optional but makes a more substantial dish; or substitute any other cured meat diced small – scraps of serrano ham, diced pancetta, streaky bacon.

Serves 3–4 as a light supper

CRUMBLE THE BREAD roughly – you don't need fine breadcrumbs – and sprinkle with salted water or stock. Leave to swell for 10 minutes, then squeeze dry.

Heat the oil in a frying pan and fry the chorizo till the fat begins to run. Stir in the breadcrumbs and garlic and let them take up all the oil. Fry gently till the breadcrumbs crisp and gild. Remove from the heat and stir in the *pimentón* (as a powdered spice made from peppers, it shouldn't be added to hot oil or it'll burn).

Migas are considered more digestible than gazpacho – bread soup in its original form, the traditional midday meal of the rural poor – and are eaten either as a late breakfast or a light evening meal, maybe with a fried egg, or as a crisp topping for an artichoke heart or cardoon (a relative of the artichoke) or chard, or any vegetable stew.

Ingredients
- 1 lb robust country bread, at least 3 days old
- About 6 tablespoons olive oil
- 3–4 garlic cloves, crushed with a little salt
- 1 soft chorizo, skinned and mashed
- 1 heaped tablespoon *pimentón* (Spanish paprika, fiery or mild, smoked or sweet)

Migas with chorizo is considered more digestible than gazpacho – bread soup in its original form, the traditional midday meal of the rural poor – and is eaten as a late breakfast or light evening meal

Salt-grilled asparagus

Grilled asparagus has a gloriously smoky flavour and keeps its firmness with no loss of juiciness. Choose fat green spears of regular size rather than the white or purple-tipped varieties.

Serves 2

BREAK THE ASPARAGUS stems at the point where they snap easily, arrange the spears in a single layer on the grill pan or in a roasting tray. Brush on all sides with a little olive oil and dust with sea salt.

Grill under a fierce heat, turning to blitz all sides, till just soft and spotted with a few black blisters. Or roast in a preheated oven at 200C/400F/Gas6 for 10–15 minutes, shaking the tray occasionally.

Serve with a jug of buttery extra virgin olive oil and a quartered lemon.

Ingredients
- 1 lb fat green asparagus
- Olive oil for brushing
- Sea salt

To serve
- Olive oil
- 1 lemon

Mayonnaise for beginners

Whisking up a mayo – maybe with a flavouring of smashed-up garlic or a mushy mix of fresh herbs – is a job for anyone who thinks they can't cook. No heat is necessary and two ingredients are all that's required, egg yolks and oil. These, when blended together, will form an emulsion.

To form the emulsion both elements must be at the same temperature and the incorporation of one into the other must be gradual. Make it once and you'll never look back.

Serves 4

Ingredients
- 2 fresh free-range eggs
- About ½ pint mild olive oil (or a mix of extra virgin and sunflower)
- About 2 tablespoons white wine vinegar or lemon juice
- Salt

REMOVE THE EGGS from the fridge and leave them beside the oil to come up to room temperature before you begin.

Crack the eggs, pull the shells apart, allow the whites to drop into a bowl (save them for meringues) and tip the yolks into another bowl. Whisk the yolks briefly to blend. Still whisking, trickle in the oil drop by drop, watching as the mixture begins to thicken. Once it looks a little paler and thicker, you can increase the flow to a thread.

patch till the emulsion reforms, and gradually work in the rest. If this doesn't work and it continues to curdle, start with a new yolk in a fresh bowl, and add the curdled mixture as slowly as at the beginning.

When the mayonnaise is beautifully shiny and stiff enough to hold its shape like soft butter, add a little salt and just enough vinegar or lemon juice to sharpen the flavour.

As for the rest, whether you eat it with seafood or serve it with raw vegetables, or as a dip for new

> *Whisking up a mayo – maybe with a flavouring of smashed-up garlic or a mushy mix of fresh herbs – is a job for anyone who thinks they can't cook. Make it once and you'll never look back*

The oil is added to the yolk, rather than the other way round, because the yolk needs to coat each particle of oil and this is easier to do when the yolk is the dominant ingredient.

Continue until a quarter of the oil has been absorbed, then change to a wooden spoon and speed up the rate of flow – it's unlikely to separate at this stage. Should this happen and it begins to look scrambled, stop beating and work a splash of boiling water into a corner, whisking vigorously at the wet

potatoes, or asparagus, or hard-boiled eggs, is up to you.

Make your mayo fresh when you need it and don't leave it out at room temperature for more than 3 hours. Store leftovers in a covered jar in the fridge for no longer than a week and let it come up to room temperature before using. Once chilled, don't whisk or stir or it will split. If this happens, stabilise the mixture by whisking a small amount into a spoonful of Dijon or any other mild mustard, an emulsifier of last resort. Then combine this mixture with your mayonnaise.

Easy hollandaise

Make this unctuous, rich, smooth, famously temperamental sauce by the melted butter method and you'll wonder what all the fuss was about. Serve with plain-cooked fish, poached eggs, steamed asparagus, new potatoes or anything else which might benefit from a dollop of joy.

Serves 2 greedy people

BLEND THE lemon juice, egg yolks and a tablespoon of warm water in a food processor for 10 seconds. Melt the butter gently till it oils (it should be bubbling but not browned). With the motor running, gradually add the hot butter to the liquidiser in a thin stream (leaving the milky residue behind in the pan) till the sauce is smooth and thick enough to coat the back of a wooden spoon. Season with a little salt, no pepper. To thicken it a little more, transfer to a bowl set over a saucepan of simmering water and whisk till the egg yolks set a little, as for a custard. To keep the sauce warm, leave it in the bowl over hot water for an hour or two, whisking occasionally.

Ingredients
- 1 tablespoon lemon juice
- 3 large egg yolks
- 6 oz unsalted butter
- Salt

Make this unctuous, rich, smooth, famously temperamental sauce by the melted butter method and you'll wonder what all the fuss was about

Green salsa

This bread-thickened sauce – you'll find variations throughout the Mediterranean – is lighter and more digestible than a mayo but serves much the same purpose. Good with anything and everything, from hot vegetables to cold chicken, hard-boiled eggs, grilled meat, plain-cooked fish (gorgeous with shellfish), baked potatoes, dressing a salad or finishing a soup. Or just eat it on its own as a dip for bread.

Makes enough for 4, but keeps well in the fridge

PROCESS ALL THE ingredients together in the liquidiser, adding the oil last in a thin stream, till smooth and thick. Or pound the onion, garlic, parsley and bread in a mortar till smooth, soften with vinegar and gradually whisk in the oil till thick. No salt or pepper, though a green chilli would add sparkle for those who like it hot. Make it ahead of time. It'll keep for 2–3 weeks stored in a screw-top jar in the fridge.

Ingredients
- 1 large Spanish onion, roughly chopped
- 2–3 garlic cloves, crushed to soften
- Large handful flat-leaf parsley, de-stalked and roughly chopped
- Small handful coriander, roughly chopped
- 3–4 mint stalks, leaves only
- 2 slices day-old bread, diced
- 2 tablespoons wine or vinegar or lemon juice
- ¼ pint extra virgin olive oil

Chocolate truffles

Make these for your best beloved on Valentine's Day, though February seems a bit chilly for romance. Roses are red, violets are blue, and if you've already spent the winter-fuel payment, so are you. Choose a high-quality chocolate with a good proportion of cocoa butter – *couverture* chocolate fits the bill.

Makes about 1 ½ lbs

Ingredients

- 1 lb high-quality dark chocolate (at least 70 per cent cocoa solids)
- ½ pint whipping cream
- Optional: 1 tablespoon brandy or whisky or crème de menthe or rum
- About 4 oz cocoa powder, sieved or squashed free of lumps

BREAK THE CHOCOLATE into small pieces in a bowl. Heat the cream in a roomy pan, remove as soon as it rises and allow to cool for a minute or two. Beat the warm cream into the chocolate with a wooden spoon till smooth. Chocolate melts at body heat, so you need to keep it warm. Beat in the optional alcohol.

Leave to cool at room temperature for 2–3 hours.

Whisk with an electric beater till the mixture becomes light and airy – for 3–4 minutes, till it begins to set. If it fails to lighten and set, the chocolate was too lean: you'll have to melt it gently over hot water with an ounce or two of unsalted butter, and whisk again.

Drop a teaspoonful of the mix into the sieved cocoa powder, making the balls as round as you can. Roll them around to coat. Set in the fridge to firm.

Then pop 'em in a cellophane bag and tie it up with red ribbon in a fancy bag. That's it.

Afghan seshtaranga

This is not, as might be supposed, a bone-cracking yoga position, but a dish of eggs and onions cooked with sugar and vinegar, popular among the Ismaili Muslims of Afghanistan says the late Lesley Blanch – she of *The Wilder Shores of Love* – who came across the recipe in Kabul in 1969. The dish would, she adds, make a splendid emergency luncheon for unexpected visitors, always a problem in the region, not least for the British army of occupation wiped out at the Kabul Pass in 1842. Same old, same old, all the way back to Tamerlane's Golden Horde.

Serves 4–6

COOK THE ONIONS in the oil till soft but not brown. Add the vinegar and simmer till mushy. When sufficiently soft and almost puréed, add sugar, salt and pepper. Stir thoroughly. While still simmering, lower the eggs carefully into dips in the onion purée. As soon as they are set, the seshtaranga is done.

Ingredients
- 10 medium onions, chunked or thickly sliced
- 2 tablespoons vegetable oil (not olive, best is grapeseed)
- ½ breakfast cup wine vinegar
- ½ breakfast cup brown sugar
- 8 eggs
- Salt and pepper

> *This is not a bone-cracking yoga position but a dish of eggs and onions cooked with sugar and vinegar, popular among the Ismaili Muslims of Afghanistan says the late Lesley Blanch, who came across the recipe in Kabul in 1969*

Chapter 8
Desserts

This chapter is all about sugar and sweetness. Sweetness, that is, as found in puddings and pies to eat with custard and cream – all those good things British cooks do best. Northerners such as ourselves love sugar because we can't get enough sunshine. Sunshine is what delivers ripeness. Ripeness is what gives us sweetness. Sweetness is addictive. Once tasted, you can't get enough of it – that's just the way it goes. And where it goes is mostly on your hips, if the diet books are right. I know very little about diets. It seems to me a couple of weeks in a famine-zone should do the trick. That, or go to bed a little hungry every night and in the morning you'll be thinner.

Nevertheless, mindful of my duty to keep abreast of all that is new in nutritional correctness, I repaired, one wet January evening, to the London Business School to bear witness to 'The Great Food Divide' – a debate on the results of a government study of the social, educational and economic differences in the eating habits of my fellow country-persons. On the platform, glamorous Suzi Leather, youthful deputy chairperson of the Food Standards Agency; by her side, Professor Tom Saunders, mustachioed professor of nutrition at King's College, London; bringing up the rear, the fourth estate's Matthew Fort, laid-back food and drink editor of the *Guardian*.

Ms Leather explained government thinking behind the free provision of apples in school to 4–6-year-olds. The professor explained the need for money to fund clinical trials on what happens when 4–6-year-olds are provided with free apples (for which a budget will also be needed). Matthew Fort, sensible fellow and a bit Italian to boot, explained that the British diet is dire, and there's damn-all to be done. We then, as befits the diet-discussing classes, repaired upstairs for refreshment – not, as might be assumed, beer and a ploughman's, but sushi and Sémillon.

And there you have it. People do what they want to do and eat what they want to eat, regardless of what anyone tells 'em – be they first, second, third or fourth estate. What we were all agreed on is that while the French do brilliant *beurre blanc* and the Italians give great ravioli, the British do the baking (see also Chapter 9: Breads, Cakes & Biscuits). And they do it regardless of income, class and education. And if they don't do it themselves, they pay someone else to do it for them – whether it's Mr Kipling or the Prince of Wales.

Which is why all our bottoms are spreading. In the meanwhile, as we all know, a little of what you fancy does you good. And too much of it makes you fat. The choice is yours.

Sicilian lemon granita

A granita, that peculiarly Sicilian version of the Middle Eastern sherbet, takes time. But what you get for your trouble is a mouth-puckering, sweetly obsessive, concentrated lemon-whack. Once tasted, nothing else will do. You'll need the juice of 8–9 lemons.

Serves 8–10

STIR THE SUGAR into half a pint of the water in a heavy-bottomed pan. Bring to the boil gently, stirring till the sugar crystals have completely dissolved. Allow to cool, stir in the lemon juice and the rest of the water: for a stronger flavour, reduce the volume of water.

Pour the mixture into an impeccably clean baking tray, and freeze for half an hour. Scrape the firm part into the soft middle, and freeze again. Repeat every half hour till firm enough to form a spoonable slush. Either serve immediately in long, chilled glasses, or store in a lidded plastic container in the freezer (take it out of the fridge 20 minutes ahead of time and give it another scrape as soon as it softens).

Serve your granita at harvest-home or whenever you feel the need for a little sunshine. A measure of vodka or gin can be incorporated for the grown-ups – but don't overdo it or it won't freeze properly.

Ingredients
- 12 oz sugar
- About 1 ½ pints water
- ½ pint freshly squeezed lemon juice

Portuguese chocolate mousse

At the Pap' Açorda, Lisbon's fashionably minimalist restaurant – all pared-down chrome, blond woodwork, white linen and impossibly beautiful waiting-staff – chocolate mousse is served from an enormous ice-frosted steel bowl and proffered to the customer on a huge wooden spoon. You can eat as much as you want, including seconds. Embarrassing – but what can a person do but accept?

Serves 4–6

BREAK THE CHOCOLATE into smallish pieces and put it in a small bowl with the butter. Set the bowl over a panful of simmering water and leave the butter and chocolate to melt together gently. The chocolate must be handled with kid gloves.

Meanwhile, in a very clean bowl, whisk the egg whites with the salt until stiff. In another bowl, whisk the egg yolks with the sugar until light and fluffy. Fold the melted chocolate into the egg yolks and then delicately fold in the whites. Tip the mixture into a metal bowl (or, more conventionally, spoon it into a glass bowl or individual ramekins) and pop it in the fridge to set. Nothing to it really.

Ingredients

- 12 oz bitter dark chocolate (at least 70 per cent cocoa solids)
- 2 oz unsalted butter
- 6 eggs, separated
- A pinch of salt
- 2 tablespoons sugar (more if you like it sweeter)

Lavender pannacotta

The secret of a perfect pannacotta, says Geraldene Holt in *Diary of a French Herb Garden* (Pavilion, 2002), is to use the absolute minimum of gelatine to give the softest possible set. Thyme or rosemary are suitable substitutes for the lavender.

Serves 6

PUT THE CREAM in a roomy saucepan and bring to the boil. Drop in the lavender tied in a scrap of cloth, and leave to infuse till cool.

Remove the lavender, bring the cream back to the boil and sprinkle the powdered gelatine over the surface, or follow the instructions on the packet if using gelatine leaves. Stir in the sugar, whisking until the crystals are perfectly dissolved. Remove from the heat. Pour into a jelly ring or 6 small individual moulds (little tumblers make a pretty shape), rinsed round with cold water. Allow to cool, and transfer to the fridge for at least 4 hours to set. The set should be light rather than firm.

To unmould, rinse a serving plate with cold water (this will allow you to slip it gently into place if necessary). Run hot water over the outside of the mould, and place the plate on top. Turn the plate and the mould over together and shake to loosen.

To finish, boil the honey in a roomy pan – it's a terrible fizzer – until reduced to half its volume. Trickle decoratively over the pannacotta and finish with any spare lavender blossoms, if you have 'em.

Ingredients
- 2–3 heads lavender
- 1 pint single cream
- 1 level teaspoon powdered gelatine or ⅓ oz leaf gelatine
- 4 level tablespoons caster sugar

Optional – to finish
- ½ jar lavender honey

Lemon curd ice cream

Dr Miriam Rothschild – flea-expert and general all-round genius – for whom I worked as an illustrator through the Eighties and Nineties, was a lifelong vegetarian and teetotaller. Eating and drinking were, however, encouraged in others, whether animal or human. She was fond of foxes, tolerating their capacity to empty her rabbit hutches, and enjoyed the company of a tawny owl which lived in her greenhouse and ate laboratory mice. She had a sweet tooth and seemed to maintain her not inconsiderable bulk on chocolate biscuits, but she would occasionally accept a helping of this ice cream.

Makes about 2 pints

TO MAKE THE lemon curd, sieve the eggs, then beat lightly. Mix in the lemon zest and the freshly squeezed juice, add the butter in small pieces and stir in the sugar. Place in the top of a double boiler or in a bowl over a pan of simmering water. Heat gently, stirring constantly, until the sugar dissolves and the mixture thickens – this takes about 20 minutes. Leave to cool.

Blend the lemon curd into the yoghurt till smooth, tip into a freezer-friendly container and freeze till firm.

Ingredients
- 3 eggs
- 3 large lemons, juice and finely grated zest
- 8 oz sugar
- 4 oz unsalted butter
- 1 pint yoghurt

135

Kirschknödel

Cherry-stuffed dumplings topped with little hats of crisp breadcrumbs, as they like them in Austria during the cherry season – especially in the famous Café Hawelka in Vienna. *Kirsche* means cherry in German. *Semmelknödel* – the generic name for bread dumplings – can be sweet or savoury. Austrian cooks can buy ready-diced stale bread in the bakery.

Serves 4–6

WORK ALL the dumpling ingredients (except the cherries) lightly together till you have a homogeneous mass. Make dumplings the size of large golf balls and push a pitted cherry in the middle (you can fill the cavity with a blanched almond or a sugar-lump instead). Poach the dumplings in plenty of just-simmering water for 10 minutes, until firm and light.

Meanwhile, fry the breadcrumbs in butter till crisp and lightly browned, then toss with sugar. Top each dumpling with a little heap of breadcrumbs.

Serve with a cherry compote, little iced glasses of Kirsch and a big jug of pouring cream.

Ingredients
The dumplings
- 8 oz diced stale bread
- 4 medium eggs
- ½ pint milk
- 2 oz plain flour
- About a dozen cherries

To finish
- 3–4 tablespoons breadcrumbs
- Large knob butter
- Sugar

CAFÉ HAWELKA

Quince and almond tart

A sophisticated winter tart from sunny Seville. The base – a crisp, buttery shortcrust pastry – is spread with cinnamon-flavoured quince paste, then baked with a topping of creamy almond custard. You can use ready-made quince paste and work in a pinch of cinnamon if fresh quinces, a winter-ripening fruit, aren't available.

Serves 6–8

MAKE THE pastry first. Sieve the flour into a bowl with the sugar. Using the tips of your fingers, rub the butter into the flour until the mixture looks like fine breadcrumbs. Work in enough egg yolk to make a softish dough – you may need a little cold water. Press into a ball, cover with clingfilm and leave in a cool place to rest for half an hour.

Preheat the oven to 200C/400F/Gas6.

Roll the pastry out with a rolling pin on a flour-dusted board with short firm strokes until you have a circle large enough to line a 7-inch tart tin. Cover the pastry with foil (shiny side down), and bake for 10 minutes. Remove the foil and bake for another 5–6 minutes, till the surface looks dry and sandy.

Meanwhile, cook the quinces in a tightly lidded pan with a tablespoonful of water till soft. Add the sugar and cinnamon, and mash over a low heat to evaporate excess moisture. Allow to cool.

Spread the quince purée over the pastry. Whizz the almond custard ingredients in the liquidiser and pour into the tart case (don't let it overflow – bake any extra in a ramekin).

Turn down the oven to 160C/325F/Gas3. Bake the tart slowly for about 1 ½ hours till gilded and set.

Ingredients
The pastry
- 12 oz flour
- 3 oz icing sugar
- 8 oz butter
- Egg yolk to bind

Quince paste
- 2 large quinces, chunked
- A pinch powdered cinnamon
- 4 tablespoons sugar

Almond custard
- 3 oz butter
- 3 oz sugar
- 6 oz blanched almonds
- Yolks of 2 eggs
- 1 teaspoon orange zest
- 1 large glass amontillado sherry or white wine

Australian apple slice

One of those good things a person needs when stuck in the outback. Apple slice – singular – is baked in a Lamington tin. A Lamington tin is flat and shallow and pretty much the same as a Swiss roll tin. Lamingtons are peculiarly Australian and are another subject altogether – I wouldn't be so foolish as to mess with Australia's sense of national identity.

Serves 6–8

PREHEAT THE OVEN to 180C/ 350F/Gas4.

Cream the butter and sugar till soft and fluffy, and gradually beat in the eggs. Mix in the flour, oats and wheat germ.

Press half the mixture into a Lamington or Swiss roll tin. Spread with the apple and sprinkle with cinnamon. Add enough milk to the remaining mixture to soften it to a consistency that drops from the spoon, and spoon it over the apples. Sprinkle with more cinnamon or sugar and bake for 30 minutes, till nicely toasted.

Ingredients
- 7 oz butter
- 8 oz brown sugar
- 2 medium eggs
- 8 oz self-raising flour
- 2 heaped tablespoons rolled oats
- 1 heaped tablespoon wheat germ
- 3–4 cooking apples, peeled, cored and chopped
- 3–4 tablespoons milk
- Some cinnamon for sprinkling

One of those good things a person needs when stuck in the outback. Apple slice is baked in a Lamington tin, which is flat and shallow. Lamingtons are peculiarly Australian

Dorset apple cake

Best made, says gardening expert Anna Pavord, with century-old apple variety Reverend W Wilks, named for the vicar of Shirley in Surrey, who invented the Shirley poppy. The Rev's 'creamy-white flesh cooks to a pale yellow froth' – though quite honestly, adds Ms Pavord, any apple will do. My own advice is to use the processor to chop the apple and replace the lard by doubling the butter.

Serves 4

Ingredients

- 8 oz plain flour
- 2 level teaspoons baking powder
- 2 oz butter
- 2 oz lard
- 4 oz brown sugar
- 1 lb apples, peeled, cored and finely chopped
- 1 medium egg, forked to blend
- A little milk

PREHEAT THE oven to 180C/350F/Gas4.

Mix the flour with the baking powder and rub in the fat. Mix in the sugar. Add the apple and mix well.

Work in the egg and enough milk to make a softish mixture which drops easily from the spoon. Spread in a buttered and base-lined cake tin measuring about 8 inches across and 1 ½ inches deep.

Bake for 45 minutes till well-risen and firm. Serve warm with custard, clotted cream, or vanilla ice cream.

Guards' pudding

A buttery bread pudding suitable for the Aga, says Ambrose Heath, writing for anxious new Aga owners in the 1930s. The Aga, you might think, defines all that is truly English about English cooking. It is, however, of Swedish invention, the brainchild of Nobel Laureate Dr Gustaf Dalén, a physicist who, after losing his sight in a laboratory accident (oops, bang, silly me), invented a cooking stove for use by the blind. The Aga, manufactured in Britain under licence in Slough, arrived on the market at the end of the 1920s. Which was just when the landed gentry, models for the prosperous urban middle classes, had lost their servants (and many of their own men) to the Great War and were obliged to instruct inexperienced newcomers. I have left Mr Heath's method, as given, admirably brief. Myself, I might drop the jam in the base of a pudding bowl instead of mixing it into the batter, but you may please yourself.

Serves 4–6

'MIX WELL TOGETHER five ounces of breadcrumbs, three ounces of caster sugar, the same of melted butter, a saltspoonful of bicarbonate of soda dissolved in a teaspoon of water, three well-beaten eggs and five tablespoonfuls of raspberry jam. Put it in a buttered mould and steam for a couple of hours.'

Ingredients
- 5 oz fresh breadcrumbs
- 3 oz caster sugar
- 3 oz unsalted butter, melted
- ½ teaspoon bicarbonate of soda
- 3 medium eggs
- 5 tablespoons raspberry jam

The Aga arrived on the market just when the landed gentry had lost their servants (and many of their own men) to the Great War and were obliged to instruct inexperienced newcomers

Lemon honeycomb jelly

Remember this? Nursery food, soft and digestible, and just right for toothless old grandads who can't be bothered to pop their teeth back in before tea. Grandchildren just love it.

Serves 4–6

PUT A LITTLE of the milk into a cup and sprinkle on the gelatine. Wait till it absorbs all the liquid and goes spongy.

Transfer the spongy liquid to a saucepan and whisk in the rest of the milk, egg yolks, the lemon zest and sugar. Bring all gently to the boil, whisking all the way. It will curdle. Remove the pan from the heat, allow to cool and remove the lemon zest.

Whisk the egg whites till stiff (stop before they go grainy) and fold them into the cooled milk mixture. Stir in the lemon juice. Transfer to a soufflé dish or jelly mould and set in the fridge for a couple of hours.

During this time, the curds will separate from the whey, producing a soft, sharp little layer of jelly on the bottom, and a honeycomb mousse on the top. Magic.

Ingredients
- 1 pint full-cream milk
- ½ oz powdered gelatine (for leaf-gelatine, follow the instructions)
- 3 lemons, finely pared zest and juice
- 3 medium eggs, separated
- 8 oz sugar

Pineapple upside-down cake

A recipe from the late Jeremy Round, founding father of the *Independent*'s cookery pages and departed before his time to the great kitchen in the sky. This is Australia's favourite granny-cake. Omit the brandy if you're catering for children, though you'll find the alcohol evaporates during the cooking.

Serves 4–6

USE A LARGE sharp stainless-steel knife to prepare the pineapple: skin, core and remove the eyes (the whiskery bits which the knife missed first time), then slice into thin rounds, allowing yourself enough to cover the base of a 9-inch diameter cake tin generously. The tin should be at least 1 ¾ inches deep and preferably non-stick.

For the topping, melt the butter in a saucepan. Add the sugar, brandy and lemon juice and stir over the heat till the mixture boils and foams. Continue to stir till it's an even, pale toffee-brown. Remove from the heat and pour into the cake tin. Arrange the pineapple slices in the sauce in a single layer, overlapping if necessary.

Preheat the oven to 190C/ 375F/Gas5.

Whizz all the cake ingredients together in the food processor until smooth and creamy, or beat them energetically by hand. Pour the mixture over the pineapple and smooth it with a spatula. Bake for 45 minutes, lowering the heat to 180C/350F/Gas4 after 30 minutes if the mixture has already set and the top looks brown. The cake is ready when it's shrunk from the sides and feels firm to the finger. Test, if you must, with a skewer pushed into the middle – I'm always a bit scared the whole thing will collapse like a deflated balloon.

Remove the cake from the oven and leave to cool for about 5 minutes. Pass a knife round the sides to make sure nothing has stuck. Place an inverted plate over the tin and then turn the whole thing over in one smooth movement. That's it. Serve with whipped cream folded with a spoonful of thick yoghurt. Yum.

Ingredients
The topping
- Half a large ripe pineapple
- 3 oz butter
- 3 oz caster sugar
- 1 tablespoon brandy
- 2 teaspoons lemon juice

The cake
- 4 oz butter
- 4 oz caster sugar
- 3 ½ oz self-raising flour
- 1 level teaspoon baking powder
- 1 rounded tablespoon roasted, skinned, ground hazelnuts
- 2 medium eggs
- 1 tablespoon brandy or lemon juice

Queen of puddings

A very grand dessert when properly presented with a jug of thick cream. Serve with a chilled glass of *Trockenbeerenauslese* – fit even for the majestic Belvedere Palace in Vienna.

Serves 4–6

PREHEAT THE OVEN to 150C/300F/Gas2.

Beat the milk with the egg yolks and 2 tablespoons of the sugar till well blended. Pour the mixture over the breadcrumbs in a bowl, turning it with a spoon.

Grease a small oval baking dish with the butter and slip it into the oven for 5 minutes till well warmed. Spread in the peach slices in a single layer. Top with the raspberries and sprinkle with a tablespoon of sugar. Cover with the soaked breadcrumbs. Bake for 30–40 minutes till the topping is set and has browned a little.

Meanwhile, make the meringue topping. Beat the egg whites till stiff, then whisk in the rest of the sugar. Pile the meringue in peaks on top of the pudding and pop it back in a hot oven for 5 minutes to brown the tops. Leave the meringue quite soft; it doesn't need to be baked crisp. Serve with cream.

Ingredients

- 1 pint creamy milk
- 2 medium eggs, separated
- 4 tablespoons caster sugar
- ½ pint fresh white breadcrumbs
- 1 tablespoon butter
- About 8 oz fresh raspberries
- 2 ripe peaches, skinned, stoned and sliced

Eliza Acton's apple charlotte

Elizabeth David described Miss Acton's elegant, erudite *Modern Cookery for Private Families*, first published in 1845, as the greatest cookery book in the English language. 'Nuff said – unless it be to add that young Isabella Beeton ruthlessly raided her predecessor's recipes but failed to acknowledge the source. 'Twas ever thus.

Serves 6–8

FIRST PREPARE THE marmalade. Put all the ingredients in a heavy pan and cook over a gentle heat till the apples are perfectly soft and jammy, beating with a wooden spoon to avoid sticking. Cook till the paste looks perfectly dry. Allow to cool.

Meanwhile, choose a medium-sized mould – a soufflé dish is fine – and line with fingers of bread dipped in melted clarified butter (to clarify butter, simply melt and avoid using the milky residue). Don't permit any gaps in the lining – if any of the apple syrup escapes, it will spoil the good appearance of the dish.

Preheat the oven to 200C/400F/Gas6.

Spoon the prepared marmalade into the bread-lined mould. Top with more bread dipped in butter. Cover with a large upturned plate or lid, or foil (shiny side down). Bake for 50–60 minutes till the crust is crisp and brown. Drain off excess butter before unmoulding onto a warm plate. Dredge thickly with caster sugar.

Ingredients
The marmalade
- 3 lbs cooking apples, pared, cored and quartered
- 6 oz unsalted butter
- 12 oz caster sugar
- 1 level teaspoon powdered cinnamon
- Juice of 1 lemon

The crust
- Very thinly sliced crustless white bread (about 12 slices)
- Melted clarified butter for dipping (2–3 oz)

To finish
- Caster sugar

Marguerite Patten's Christmas pudding

Ms Patten points out that the steamed Christmas pudding is bit of a Johnny-come-lately, being unknown in Britain till the seventeenth century. Before that, she explains, we ate plum porridge much like that known in Nordic countries. This recipe is tried and tested by the author herself and is not suitable, she says, for the microwave. No need to make it weeks ahead – the long cooking ensures the flavours mature well, even when the pudding is freshly made.

Makes 2 large puddings, each serving 6–8

> *The steamed Christmas pudding is a bit of a Johnny-come-lately, being unknown in Britain till the seventeenth century. Before that, we ate plum porridge, much like that known in Nordic countries*

MIX ALL THE ingredients together in a bowl. Leave to stand overnight. Grease two 2½-pint ovenproof basins and spoon in the mixture. Cover with well-greased greaseproof paper and foil. Put a central pleat in both covers so the pudding will not split the covering. Steam each pudding over boiling water for 5–6 hours, making sure the pans do not boil dry – top up with boiling water if necessary. When the puddings are cooked, remove the damp covers at once. When cold, cover with fresh dry greaseproof paper and foil. Store in a cool dry place. On Christmas day, steam the pudding for 2 hours. Serve with custard, brandy butter or Cumberland rum butter (see page 146).

Ingredients
- 4 oz suet or butter, grated or melted
- 4 oz glacé cherries (optional), chopped
- 4 oz mixed crystallized peel, chopped
- 4 oz each dried apricots and prunes, chopped
- 4 oz almonds, chopped
- 1 medium carrot, peeled and grated
- 1 medium cooking apple, peeled and grated
- 3 oz plain flour
- 6 oz fresh breadcrumbs
- ½ teaspoon each ground cinnamon, nutmeg, allspice
- 4 oz soft dark brown sugar
- 6 oz each currants and sultanas
- 12 oz raisins
- 1 teaspoon each grated orange and lemon zest
- 1 tablespoon each lemon and orange juice
- 1 tablespoon black treacle
- 8 fl oz beer, stout or milk
- 2 large eggs, forked to blend

Cumberland rum butter

Rum butter is so popular in Cumberland, says Marguerite Patten, that it's made throughout the year and served on bread, in sponges and on pancakes. Chill it but don't freeze it. You can use more rum if you wish.

Serves 6

CREAM THE BUTTER till soft and fluffy, add the sugar and beat well (if you use demerara, don't expect it to be smooth). Gradually beat in the rum and optional spices. Nothing to it, really.

Ingredients

- 4 oz unsalted butter
- 6 oz demerara or soft brown sugar
- 2 tablespoons rum
- Optional: a pinch each of ground cinnamon and nutmeg

"Rum butter is so popular in Cumberland that it's made throughout the year and served on bread, in sponges and on pancakes"

Pim's frangipane apple pie

Pim Techamuanvivit, megastar of the foodie blogosphere (keep up at the back), was born in Bangkok, served time as a science-techie in San Francisco's silicone valley, and then became famous as a web-cook. Believe me, she's huge. Actually, she's tiny. Slender as a stalk of lemon-grass and pretty as a picture, even with chopsticks sticking out of her mouth. *The Foodie Handbook* (Conran, 2009) is Pim's 'almost definitive' guide to gastronomy. Here's her gloriously buttery, sugary, nutty apple pie. Take your time. No short cuts.

Serves 6–8

FIRST MAKE THE pastry. Measure the flour onto a clean work surface. Cut the butter into large chunks and place them on top in a single layer. Begin to blend the flour and butter together by pressing down on the pile with the heel of your hand. Use a pastry scraper to flip some of the dough over the pile. Continue pressing and scraping till the butter looks like very fine flakes pressed into the flour.

Now use your fingertips to mix the dough till the flakes are slightly broken and you have a combination of fine flakes and crumbs. Pour the cold water into the dough in a thin stream and use your fingertips to distribute it evenly. Use the scraper to pick up the dough and press it over itself until you have a cohesive lump of dough. Gather it into a ball, press it into a dish and wrap in clingfilm. Let it rest in the fridge for 30 minutes before you roll it out in a rectangle on a floured board. Fold the dough in thirds towards the middle. Turn it 90 degrees, fold it and roll again. Repeat a couple more times. Fold in thirds again, wrap in clingfilm and leave to rest for another hour in the fridge. The pastry is now ready to roll as a tart base. Cut it into 2 equal pieces and roll one piece out to fit a 10-inch tart tin (save the other piece for another day – it freezes perfectly).

Meanwhile, make the frangipane: toast the almonds on a baking sheet in the oven at 180C/350F/Gas4 for 10–12 minutes till lightly browned. Cool to room temperature, transfer to a food processor, add the sugar and pulse to a fine powder. Add the butter and pulse again to blend. Drop in the egg and continue to pulse till it comes together.

Preheat the oven to 190C/375F/Gas5.

Spread the frangipane in a thick layer on the pastry base, top with apple slices arranged in concentric rings and bake for about 45 minutes, till the crust is golden and the topping is springy and brown.

Ingredients

The pastry
- 9 oz plain flour
- 8 oz salted butter
- 2 fl oz water

The frangipane
- 3 oz whole almonds (blanched or not, as you please)
- 2 ½ oz sugar
- 3 oz butter, room temperature
- 1 egg, forked to blend

The apples
- 3–4 tart green apples, peeled, cored and sliced

Chapter 9
Breads, Cakes & Biscuits

There's one very good reason to bake your own bread. British bread, say our fellow Europeans, is now the nastiest in all Europe. Which can come as something of a shock to those of us who've always known that baking is what the British cook does best – whether Scots, Irish, Welsh or English, from crumpets to fruit cake, shortbread, fairy cakes, and the everyday loaf, there's nothing to beat the British.

Not any longer. If you ask artisan baker Andrew Whitley why things have come to such a pass, he will tell you in a nanosecond: the Chorleywood Bread Process. CBP is a method of bread manufacture which, in combination with ADD (activated dough development – sinister, don't you think?), relies on a much reduced preparation time and the use of a lower-protein wheat, along with assorted enzymes, emulsifiers and 'processing aids' of varying degrees of permitted toxicity, to produce a bread of astonishing puffiness and lightness. The process first appeared in the early 1960s, something of a low point in the diet of these islands, when we had enough to eat but we'd forgotten how to cook it. Cheap bread was what the customers wanted – which suited the industrial manufacturers just fine, not least because people soon forget how good the real thing tastes. But that was before anyone had assessed the price in increased health problems – not all of them the result of too much fat and sugar.

More than 80 per cent of our bread is now made by the Chorleywood method. And if that's not enough to get you kneading your own – not to mention baking your own cakes and cookies with ingredients which don't need to identify themselves by e-numbers – there's increasing evidence that industrially processed baked goods are at the root of a great many forms of food intolerance, some more serious than others, all of which can be avoided by reclaiming control of the raw materials.

So get baking. It's easier than you think. One consequence of closer trading ties with our European neighbours is a resurgence of interest in home baking – led, it must be admitted, by workers from elsewhere, Germany in particular, where anyone baking their own bread is more than likely to mill their own grain. And if you mill your own grain, you're more than likely to raise your bread with your own leavening kept from one batch to another. Which is just about all you need to start your own bakery.

The Grant loaf

Doris Grant, founding mother of the safe food movement in the 1950s and vigorous campaigner for higher nutritional standards in the British diet, published this acclaimed recipe towards the end of World War Two. Her instructions for a healthy, fortifying wholemeal loaf which required no kneading came at a time when working wives, fed up with the anaemic national loaf but unable to spend much time in the kitchen, were ready to try their hand at home baking. Sounds familiar.

Makes three 2-lb loaves

FIRST, SET READY your three loaf tins, well-greased.

In a roomy bowl, warm the flour a little in a very low oven – or set it out in the summer sunshine – and mix in the salt. In a small bowl, mix the 3 tablespoons of warm water with the yeast and whisk till completely dissolved. Whisk in the sugar or honey or treacle. Leave to froth – it'll take about 15 minutes.

Pour the frothy liquid into a well in the flour and add the two pints of warm water. Mix to a dough with the hook of your hand. Work it till smooth and elastic enough to leave the sides of the bowl – don't worry if it's still a bit sticky.

Divide into 3 equal pieces, knead each piece into a fat little bolster, tucking the seam underneath, and transfer to the loaf tins. Cover with a clean cloth and leave to rise for 30 minutes in a warm draught-proof corner.

Preheat the oven to 200C/400F/Gas6.

Bake the loaves for 40 minutes till well-risen and brown. Tip them out of the tin and give the base a tap. If it sounds hollow, the bread is ready. If not, pop them back in the oven for another 5–10 minutes.

The dough makes a very good pizza base: pat out thinly into rounds, top as you please and bake in the highest possible oven.

Ingredients

- 3 lbs stoneground wholemeal flour
- 2 teaspoons salt
- 3 tablespoons warm water at blood heat
- 3 level teaspoons dried yeast (if using easy-blend, follow the instructions on the packet)
- 3 rounded teaspoons dark brown sugar or honey or black treacle
- 2 pints warm water at blood heat

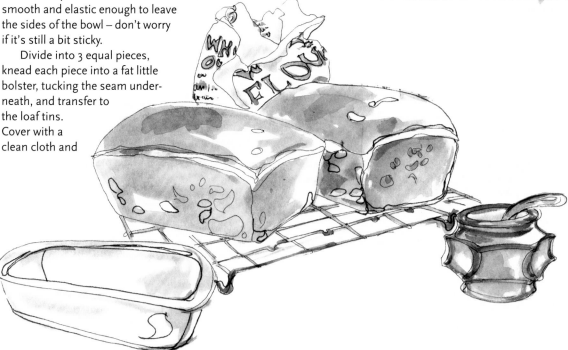

Everyday slow-raise bread

Slow-rise takes time, surprisingly little effort and tastes terrific. Success guaranteed when you follow these instructions from artisan baker Andrew Whitley, founder of the Village Bakery, scourge of the supermarket ready-sliced and author, by way of setting the record straight, of *Bread Matters* (Fourth Estate, 2009). Measurements are precise and should be followed as given – I've left them metric: the baker knows his business. Consider the finished dough suitable for anything from ciabatta to crumpets.

Makes a 1-lb loaf

THE SPONGE: Dissolve the yeast in the water. Add the flours and mix to a soft sponge – no need to mix vigorously. Put the sponge in a bowl large enough to allow for a 3-times expansion. Cover with a lid or plastic bag to conserve moisture. Leave to ferment at room temperature for 16–48 hours. The sponge will rise up and collapse as the yeast cells multiply and lactic and acetic acids begin to develop.

THE FINAL DOUGH: The water must be warm enough to bring the mixture up to 27C. Mix all the ingredients together and knead until the dough is stretchy and silky. Cover and allow to rise for an hour or so. The dough is now suitable for moulding into loaves, slipper-shaped ciabatta or whatever savoury bread takes your fancy.

Allow 1–2 hours for a second rising, then slip it gently into the oven. The usual bread baking temperature is 180C/350F/Gas4, though the heat can be higher – 190C/375F/Gas5 – if the bread is flat rather than loaf-shaped.

Baking time will be from 40–60 minutes, depending on size and thickness. The loaf is ready when it's well-shrunk from the sides, brown and well-risen on top, and the underside sounds hollow when you tap it.

Ingredients
The sponge
(total finished weight 303 g)
- 3 g fresh yeast
- 150 g water (at 20C)
- 75 g strong white flour
- 75 g stoneground wholemeal flour

The final dough
(total finished weight 574 g)
- 225 g sponge (from above)
- 150 g strong white flour
- 75 g stoneground wholemeal flour
- 4 g sea salt
- 15 g olive oil
- 105 g water

One good turn deserves another: a basic bread dough can be diluted to make a pouring batter to be cooked on top of the stove as griddle-cakes such as pikelets and crumpets

Crumpets

One good turn deserves another: a basic bread dough can be enriched with butter, egg and/or dried fruit to make fruit breads, the original celebration cakes, or diluted to make a pouring batter to be cooked on top of the stove as griddle-cakes such as pikelets and crumpets.

Makes a dozen

DILUTE THE DOUGH to a pouring consistency with 50 ml (2 oz) warm water. Leave to ferment again for 1–2 hours.

Heat a heavy raw iron griddle, wipe the surface with an oily cloth and have ready a ring roughly the diameter of two hands joined to make a circle. Pour in a thumb's width of the batter and bake till the underside is brown and the top is just set. Flip over and toast for a couple of minutes on the other side. Continue till all the batter is used up.

Ingredients

- 500g (1 lb) ready-risen bread dough (as in previous recipe, see page 151)

Ethiopian flatbreads

Crumpet batter can be used to prepare *injeera*, a floppy, bubbly scooping bread about the size of a large dinner plate traditionally made from teff (*Eragrostis abyssinica*) – a place-specific member of the millet family no bigger than a poppy seed which, when ripened, flops earthwards and must be harvested by hand. Never altered by cultivation, teff crops 4 or 5 times a year and is unsuitable for machine harvesting, making it hard to exploit commercially. It is, however, capable of serving as a 'sole' food (sustainable, organic, local, ethical food), one of three miracle grains which might one day feed the world (two others are amaranth and quinoa). Experimental crops are now being grown on the plains of Oregon, which may well be very good news indeed.

Makes 6–8, depending on the size of the bakestone or frying pan

YOU MAY NEED to mix in a little more warm water to ensure a suitably runny pancake-like batter which flows smoothly onto its bakestone.

Preheat a large frying pan or griddle, rub with a scrap of cloth dipped in oil or butter, and wait till a faint blue haze rises.

Pour the batter round the edge of the pan and continue clockwise in a circle till you reach the middle. Wait for 3–4 minutes, till the top looks dry and bubbly. Transfer to a clean cloth to keep the pancake warm.

Provide each person with one bread to serve as a plate and another, rolled up into a little bolster, to serve as a scoop. Each person dots the plate-bread with little heaps of fiery chicken curry (see recipe page 65), plain-cooked dhal, vegetable curry flavoured with ginger, a hard-boiled egg and a little dab of soft white curd cheese – some or all of these, according to the skill of the cook and the purse of the household.

Ingredients
- 1 ½ pints ready-made crumpet batter (as previous recipe, see page 152)
- Oil or butter for greasing

Indian roti

Roti is the generic name throughout India for all unleavened bread. Confusion can arise since such breads, as with Middle Eastern pittas, come by regional names and are made with variable blends of flours to recipes which differ as much, say, as the French croissant from the California sourdough. Flatbreads serve as both plate and scoop and are eaten with small amounts of other things – mostly vegetarian, since devout Hindus eat no meat. A meal without some form of flatbread would be unthinkable as well as impractical, since only the Westernised use cutlery. Eating is done with the fingers – right hand only – carefully washed before every meal to ensure that the eating instrument is clean, a practical precaution in the tropics. In the home, scooping breads, roti (with their varied names and recipes), are the centrepiece of the meal, cooked to order, the responsibility of the senior matron or her favoured deputy, and prepared fresh in batches throughout the meal to ensure they're eaten hot. When the dough is finished, so is the meal.

Makes 16 breads

TOSS THE FLOUR with the salt and work in enough water to make a softish dough. Oil your hand and knead the dough-ball till smooth. Divide it into 16 pieces. Dust a board with flour and roll out each piece into a thin round, diameter about 5 inches.

Heat a bakestone or griddle or heavy frying pan and bake a round at a time till the edges curl. Flip it over and bake the other side till air bubbles form. Remove with tongs and hold in a gas flame for a few seconds till it puffs and splits. Brush with melted ghee or butter and pile in a clean napkin to keep warm. Serve with a soupy dhal and a vegetable curry.

Ingredients
- 1lb stoneground wholemeal flour
- 1 teaspoon salt
- 1 teaspoon vegetable oil

To finish
- 2–3 tablespoons softened ghee or melted unsalted butter

Easter breads

The Easter breads of the Catholic and Orthodox tradition are made with a yeast-raised fine white bread dough enriched with eggs and butter (or lard or oil). They do, however, come in many forms, each with its own rationale. Some are curled into a ring and studded with eggs in their shells, as in Spain and Portugal. Others are baked in the form of a tall crown, as the Russian *babka*. Still others, in parts of Germany and northern Italy, come in the form of animals or human figures with unshelled eggs popped into heads or bellies. Some, a common form in Eastern Europe, are plaited like the Jewish Sabbath bread, the *challa*. Within these basic shapes, other refinements are possible. Among the Ruthenes of Slovakia, Ukrainians by descent, the Russian crown is combined with the Slovakian plait.

Serves a dozen

SIEVE THE FLOUR and salt into a warm bowl. Work the yeast with the sugar till it liquidises, then whisk in the warm milk, melted butter and forked-up egg yolks. Pour into a well in the flour and work with the hook of your hand till it forms a soft sticky mass. Whisk the egg whites and work them in – the more air, the better. Tip onto a floured board and knead thoroughly till you have a soft smooth dough – you may need a little more milk or flour. Drop the dough-ball back in the bowl, cover with clingfilm and leave to rise for an hour or two in a warm place, till doubled in size.

Knuckle the dough down with a closed fist to distribute the air bubbles, and cut into six equal pieces. Roll each piece into a short fat rope, and make two plaits, pinching the ends together with a damp finger. Coil the plaits into 2 tall round cake tins, well-buttered and lined with greaseproof paper. Brush with a little egg and milk, and set to rise for another 30–40 minutes, till the dough regains its volume.

Preheat the oven to 200C/400F/Gas6.

Bake the breads for 35–40 minutes, till well-risen and brown (the base should sound hollow when you tap it). Transfer to a rack to cool.

You can use the same dough for hot cross buns, our own version of an Easter bread. Just work a handful of raisins and a pinch of ground cinnamon into the dough after the first rising. Cut it into a dozen pieces, form into balls, mark them with a cross in any way which works (flour and water paste perhaps), transfer to a buttered baking sheet and set to rise again. Bake for 10–15 minutes at 220C/450F/Gas8. As soon as they come out of the oven, glaze them with sugar syrup – sugar bubbled to a syrup in its own volume of water.

Ingredients
- 2 ½ lbs strong white flour
- 1 teaspoon salt
- 1 tablespoon sugar
- 2 oz fresh yeast
- 2 eggs, separated
- 1 pint full-cream milk, warmed to hand-heat
- 2 oz unsalted butter, just melted

Cinnamon streusel cake

A rich buttery dough-cake enriched with eggs to serve warm from the oven – delicious with raspberries and cream in summer or stewed apples in the winter. They make an excellent version in Café Demel in Vienna, where I sketched the café's lavish interior (below).

Serves 6

MAKE THE DOUGH first. Dissolve the yeast in the warm milk. Stir in the sugar and leave the mixture to stand for a few minutes. Beat in the eggs, the lemon zest and the melted butter. Gradually knead in enough flour (mix it with the salt) to give you a soft, smooth, elastic dough. Work the dough into a ball, drop it back in the bowl, cover with clingfilm and set in a warm place for an hour or two, until well-puffed. A rich dough takes longer to rise than a plain one.

Punch the dough with your fist to distribute the air bubbles, drop it onto a buttered, lightly floured baking tin – a Swiss roll tin will take this amount of dough nicely – flatten to fit the tin, cover as before and leave to rise again for another 30 minutes.

Meanwhile prepare the topping (the streusel): use a knife to chop the ingredients together until they look crumbly.

Brush the dough with melted butter and sprinkle thickly with the streusel.

Preheat the oven to 190C/375F/Gas5.

Bake the cake for 30–40 minutes, until the dough is firm and the topping is crunchy and golden. If the top browns too fast, turn the oven down a notch – after the first 10 minutes, there's no danger the cake will collapse.

Ingredients
The cake
- 1 oz fresh yeast
- ⅛ pint warm milk
- 2 tablespoons sugar
- 2 eggs, well beaten
- 4 oz butter, just melted
- Zest of 1 lemon
- About 8 oz flour
- ¼ teaspoon salt

The topping (streusel)
- 2 oz butter, chilled and chopped
- 1 oz flour
- 1 oz ground almonds
- 6 oz sugar
- 1 tablespoon powdered cinnamon
- 1 tablespoon melted butter for brushing

DEMEL – VIENNA

Jenny's heavenly coffee cake

This pecan- and sugar-topped ring-cake with a sticky toffee centre is finger-licking good. Coffee cakes, says my American friend Jennifer Skiff, whose speciality this is, are cakes which are eaten with coffee rather than cakes which actually taste of coffee. Which fits in with the general confusion over English scones being American biscuits, and English biscuits being American cookies, and muffins being those puffy things which look like overblown cupcakes that you get for breakfast in Starbucks. You can freeze the leftovers, says Jenny – ex-CNN presenter, now author of inspirational self-help manuals – except you won't need to because there won't be any.

Serves 6–8

FIRST MAKE the streusel. Throw the pecans (or walnuts) in the food processor and hit the pulse button 3 times, leaving the nuts chunky.

Change to the mixing paddle and toss in all the ingredients, making sure to cut the butter into little pieces. Mix but don't overmix or the butter will cream when it has to stay lumpy. Reserve the streusel while you make the batter.

Cream the butter, sugar and vanilla together in the processor. Add the eggs one at a time, still mixing. Add salt, baking soda and baking powder, crushing it together first with your fingers to eliminate lumps, and scraping the side of the bowl with a spatula. Add alternate spoonfuls of flour and yoghurt until everything's in.

Preheat the oven to 175C/350F/Gas4.

Butter a large ring-tin, pour in half the batter and sprinkle with half of the pecan mix. Pour in the rest of the batter and finish with the remaining pecan mix.

Bake the cake for about 1 ¾ hours, or until the topping is crispy brown, nearing burnt. Check with a skewer – there should be no liquid batter, but expect to see runny brown sugar. Allow to cool for an hour. Be patient. Now loosen the edges with a spatula and flip it out of its mould.

Ingredients
Streusel topping and filling
- 12 oz light brown sugar
- 1 tablespoon ground cinnamon
- 8 oz chopped pecans (or walnuts)
- 4 oz refrigerated butter

Cake batter
- 2 oz butter at room temperature
- 8 oz granulated sugar
- 2 teaspoons vanilla extract
- 4 large eggs
- ½ teaspoon salt
- 1 teaspoon baking soda
- 1 ¼ teaspoons baking powder
- 8 oz thick Greek yoghurt
- 10 oz plain flour

CASABLANCA MOSQUE HASSAN II

Casablanca orange cake

A cut-and-come-again cake, a good keeper even in a hot climate, from the most Frenchified area of Morocco (even Casablanca's Hassan II Mosque, the largest mosque in Morocco, was designed by a French architect, Michel Pinseau). The recipe includes the pulp of whole oranges and is enriched with oil rather than butter, a common substitution in olive-growing regions of the Mediterranean. You'll need small thin-skinned unwaxed fruits: marmalade oranges are perfect. If waxed, scrub well to remove the shiny coating. The recipe also works well with lemons, particularly if you replace a couple of tablespoons of flour with ground almonds.

Serves 6–8

PREHEAT THE OVEN to 180C/350F/Gas4.

Slice off and discard the tops and bottoms of the oranges and chunk the rest, skin and all. Scoop out and discard the pips. Use a processor to reduce the orange chunks to a thick purée. Add the oil slowly till well mixed. Reserve.

Whisk the eggs till very thick and lemon-coloured. Beat in the sugar spoonful by spoonful till the mixture is pale and fluffy. Keep going till it's really light and white.

Sift the flour with the baking powder and salt. Sieve into a bowl. Fold a third of the flour into the egg mixture, followed by a third of the orange mixture. Add another third of flour, then another third of orange. Continue with the remainder.

Butter and line with greaseproof paper a medium-sized loaf-tin – 10 inches x 4 inches is about right. Tip the mixture into the tin.

Bake for 50–60 minutes (check after 40 minutes and turn the oven down a little if necessary) until well-risen and shrunk from the sides. Remove and allow to cool a little before you tip it out onto the baking rack. Store in an airtight tin when perfectly cool. Great for breakfast with butter and marmalade.

Ingredients
• 2 small unwaxed oranges
• 4 tablespoons light olive oil (virgin is too strong)
• 4 large eggs
• 10 oz granulated sugar
• 10 oz plain flour
• 1 teaspoon baking powder
• ½ teaspoon salt
• A little butter for greasing

Rich chocolate cake

A luscious sponge cake made with ground almonds rather than flour. Almonds were first planted in the gardens of Granada by the Moors, and sponge cakes are known in Italy as *pan di Spagna* – 'Spanish bread'. Blame it on the Borgias, a sybaritic lot.

Serves 6–8

PREHEAT THE OVEN to 180C/350F/Gas4.

Melt the chocolate with the coffee, butter and sugar in a bowl set over a pan of simmering water (or melt in the microwave). Remove from the heat, stir and leave to cool a little while you whisk the egg whites till they hold soft peaks. Beat the egg yolks into the melted chocolate mixture and fold in the ground almonds. Then fold in the whisked whites – add only one spoonful at first, so that the mixture lightens and is ready to accept the rest.

Butter a cake tin, diameter 9 inches (preferably one with a removable base), and dust lightly with flour or line with greaseproof paper. Tip the mixture into the tin, spreading it to make a flat surface.

Bake for 40–50 minutes, till well-risen and firm to the finger. Let it cool before you turn it out. Dust the top with icing sugar, a light dusting rather than the full snowstorm – just enough to emphasise the lusciously dark crust while disguising the cracks.

Ingredients

- 8 oz bitter black chocolate (look for 70 per cent cocoa solids)
- 1 tablespoon strong coffee
- 4 oz unsalted butter
- 6 oz caster sugar
- 6 oz ground almonds
- 6 eggs, separated

> *A luscious sponge cake made with ground almonds rather than flour. Almonds were first planted in the gardens of Granada by the Moors*

Simnel cake

This is the Great British Fruitcake, topped and middled with marzipan, baked by Victorian housemaids to take home to their mums on Mothering Sunday. As for the curious name, theories abound, but the most likely is the most prosaic, *simila* being Latin for fine white flour, the main ingredient. Make your own marzipan – the bought stuff won't hold its shape in the oven.

Serves a party

PICK OVER the fruit and nuts and toss in a little flour (this helps prevent the solids sinking to the bottom of the cake). Beat the sugar and butter together until light and fluffy – the more you beat, the easier the adding of the eggs. Beat in the eggs one by one, stirring in a spoonful of flour if it looks like curdling. Sieve in the flour with the salt, add the powdered almonds, and fold gently. Fold in the fruit, nuts, spices and molasses, and enough brandy or milk to give a soft mixture which drops easily from the spoon.

Preheat the oven to 170C/325F/Gas 3. Line an 8-inch cake tin with buttered paper. Mix the marzipan ingredients, adding a tablespoon of water to make a softish paste. Roll or pat the marzipan into a disc which would just cover the base of the tin – use icing for dusting to stop sticking. Reserve.

Spoon half the cake mixture into the tin. Level it out and top with the marzipan disc. Spoon in the rest of the mixture and set aside for half an hour to allow the fruit to swell.

Bake for 2 ½–3 hours until the cake is well-browned and firm to the touch. If it browns too quickly, cover the top with greaseproof paper. Leave to cool a little before you tip it out of the tin.

To finish, brush the top with apricot jam and lay on another disc of marzipan (same recipe), saving enough to make 13 little balls. Stick 12 apostles round the edge and pop Jesus in the middle. Store in an airtight tin.

Ingredients
- 2 oz blanched almonds
- 6 oz prunes, stoned and chopped
- 8 oz sultanas
- 8 oz raisins
- 4 oz crystallised peel
- 4 oz crystallised cherries
- 6 oz butter
- 6 oz soft brown sugar
- 4 eggs
- 6 oz self-raising flour
- ½ teaspoon salt
- 2 teaspoons powdered almonds
- 1 teaspoon powdered cinnamon
- ½ teaspoon grated nutmeg
- 1 tablespoon molasses or black treacle
- 1 small glass brandy or milk

The marzipan
- 8 oz ground almonds
- 2 tablespoons icing sugar
- 1 large egg yolk

Caribbean black cake

Sumptuously dark and rich with fruit, butter and eggs, black cake is the special occasion cake of the Caribbean – baked for Easter and weddings as well as Christmas. Its colour and distinctive flavour depend on the inclusion of burnt sugar, essence of which can be bought in West Indian grocery stores. Molasses is a possible substitute, or burn your own sugar syrup – start with brown sugar and very little water, stir till dissolved and keep going till it's black and bitter.

Makes 2 large cakes (black cake is a good keeper)

CHOP ALL THE fruit thoroughly and bottle up in a large jar – or put in a covered bowl – with the sherry/port and rum. Leave to macerate for at least a couple of weeks.

When you are ready to bake, line a couple of clip-sided 9-inch diameter cake tins with well-buttered paper.

Preheat the oven to 180C/350F/Gas4.

Cream the butter with the brown sugar until light and fluffy. Stir in the fruit and its soaking liquor, the vanilla, nutmeg and cinnamon. Beat in the eggs and work in the flour sieved with the baking powder. Stir in the burnt sugar plus a little milk if the mixture's too stiff to drop easily from the spoon. Divide the mixture between the tins.

Bake for 1–1 ¼ hours, till firm and shrunk from the sides. Keep an eye on the colour, and if necessary cover the top with greaseproof paper halfway through to stop burning. Let the cakes cool a little before you tip them out and peel off the paper.

Store 'em till you're ready – they'll develop nicely in the tin. Finish, if appropriate, with a simple white icing made with well-sieved icing sugar, enough egg white to bind and a drop of almond essence for flavour.

Ingredients
The fruit
- 1 lb raisins
- 1 lb prunes
- 1 lb currants
- 1 lb dried figs
- 1 lb glacé cherries
- 12 oz mixed peel
- 1 bottle sweet sherry or white port
- 1 whole bottle dark rum (fabulous, eh?)

The cake mixture
- 1 lb butter
- 1 lb dark brown sugar
- 1 tablespoon vanilla extract
- 1 teaspoon grated nutmeg
- 1 teaspoon powdered cinnamon
- 12 medium eggs
- 1 ¼ lbs flour
- 3 teaspoons baking powder
- 4 tablespoons essence of burnt sugar (bought/home-made)

'Dottie Davies' lemon drizzle cake

Dorothy Davies is the *nom de plume* of my good friend Frances Jones Davies, editor of *Cambria* magazine, Wales' most intelligent and independence-minded glossy – and no, it's not a supporter of the Prince of Wales. Everyone knows how to make this, says Dottie, except they don't – and it's the nicest cake on the Welsh tea-table.

Serves 4–6

PREHEAT THE OVEN to 170C/325F/Gas3.

Beat the butter with the sugar with a wooden spoon or in the food mixer till light and pale. Beat in the eggs, a dribble at a time. Fold in the flour with a metal spoon or spatula, adding the lemon juice and zest, and a little milk if necessary to soften to dropping consistency.

Tip into a lined, buttered cake tin, diameter 7–8 inches, or a 2-lb loaf tin (roughly 10 x 5 inches). Bake for 40–50 minutes, till well-risen and shrunk from the sides.

Meanwhile, prepare the drizzle: melt the sugar in the lemon juice on a low heat or in the microwave. Pour the syrup into and over the cake as soon as it comes out of the oven.

Ingredients	For the drizzle
• 6 oz softened butter	• Juice of 2 lemons
• 6 oz caster sugar	• 4 oz caster sugar
• 2 large eggs, forked to blend	
• 6 oz self-raising flour	
• Juice and zest of 1 lemon	
• 2–3 tablespoons milk	

Maw Broon's sponge sandwich

Grannies and grandads and all oldies who take their responsibilities seriously would be well advised in these straightened times to get the next generation into the kitchen. Scrap the stuff about making smiley faces on the pizza and take advice from *Maw Broon's Cooking with Bairns* (Waverley Books, 2010). Ms Broon – aka the thoroughly grown-up Catherine Brown – delivers reliable recipes in cartoon form. One of my grandchildren test-drove this recipe for the classic Victoria sponge, and found it easy-peasy. I've left the measurements metric because the grandchild can't handle pounds and ounces. Oldies will know that 250 g is pretty much the same thing as 8 oz. The method is unusual but works brilliantly.

Makes 2 cakes

PREHEAT THE OVEN to 180C/350F/Gas4. Have ready 2 cake tins, diameter 20 cm, buttered and lined with greaseproof paper.

Warm the eggs: put into a bowl of hot but not boiling water. Leave for 2 minutes. Take out the eggs and break into a measuring jug. Whisk till thoroughly mixed. Sift the self-raising flour, baking powder and sugar into a mixing bowl and beat with the electric beater for 20 seconds. Make a well in the centre of the flour and sugar mixture. Add the softened butter, most of the egg and the vanilla, and beat for 60 seconds, when the mixture should change to a lighter colour and become thick and creamy. Add the remaining egg and beat for another 30 seconds. The mixture should have a soft dropping consistency. Add some milk if it's too stiff. Put the mixture into the prepared tins. Use the spatula to get all of the mixture out of the bowl and to level the tops.

Bake for 40–50 minutes if you're baking two cakes, or for 60 minutes if you're baking one large cake. Test with a skewer or a sharp knife to see if the cakes are ready. The skewer or knife should come out clean. Remove the sponges from their tins and cool on a rack.

Spread jam on the underside of one sponge. Place the underside of the other sponge on top of the jam and dust the top with sieved icing sugar. Or fill and spread with butter icing. For this you'll need 175 g butter at room temperature beaten till light and fluffy with 250 g icing or caster sugar.

Ingredients

- 4 large eggs
- 250 g self-raising flour
- 1 teaspoon baking powder
- 250 g caster sugar
- 250 g butter
- 1 teaspoon vanilla essence
- 1–2 tablespoons milk
- Jam for filling
- Icing sugar for dusting

Pecan coconut energy slices

An Australian goodie to be packed in your pocket when you're off to the gym. They keep well in an airtight tin, so make double portions and store 'em up for a rainy day.

Makes about a dozen

MIX ALL THE dry ingredients till well-blended. Melt the honey and butter together. Stir the wet mixture into the dry, working in the eggs till well-blended. Press into a buttered Swiss roll tin or similar.

Preheat the oven to 180C/350F/Gas4.

Bake for 25–30 minutes till golden brown. Cut into fingers or squares and transfer to a baking rack to cool. Store in an airtight tin.

Ingredients

- 4 oz chopped pecans
- 4 oz rolled oats
- 4 oz sultanas
- 2 oz wholewheat flour
- 2 oz bran
- 2 oz shredded coconut
- 2 oz muscovado sugar
- 2 oz sesame seeds
- 1 tablespoon honey
- 4 oz butter
- 2 eggs, forked to blend

An Australian goodie to be packed in your pocket when you're off to the gym. They keep well in an airtight tin, so make double portions and store them up for a rainy day

Fruit and oat slice

Fortifying stuff from the home cooks of Clare Valley in South Australia, where wine-makers are contemplating great purple drifts of desert-loving wild flowers on land where vines once flourished. The dry stems and crisp flowers are, however, appreciated by sheep and honey-bees, which is not much compensation for grape growers bedevilled by water quotas as the Murray River loses flow. The measurements are Australian: a cup can be read as a standard coffee-mug.

Makes about a dozen

THIS RECIPE IS prepared in 2 parts, topping and base.

To make the topping, bring the fruit, nuts and spice to the boil in ½ cup water, allow to cool and mix in the coconut and the egg.

To make the base, melt the sugar, butter and syrup together and mix it into the flour and oats.

Preheat the oven to 180C/350F/Gas4.

Spread the base into a buttered baking tray and top with the fruit-nut mix. Bake for 30 minutes, till set and firm. Cut into squares or fingers.

Ingredients

- 1 pint mixed fruit and nuts
- 1 teaspoon mixed spice
- 6 tablespoons shredded coconut
- 1 egg, forked to blend
- 4 tablespoons brown sugar
- 4 oz butter
- ¼ pint golden syrup
- ½ cup plain flour
- 1 cup rolled oats

Sydney

Anzac biscuits

Call it an early version of the breakfast bar, this fruit-and-nut parkin was originally devised by Australian wives to include in food parcels sent to their soldier husbands during World War Two. I have left the measurements Aussie-style: use a standard coffee-mug as the measuring cup.

Makes a dozen

COMBINE THE OATS, flour, sugar and coconut.

Melt the butter with the syrup. Mix the soda with the boiling water and add the melted butter mix. Fold in the dry ingredients till well-blended.

Preheat the oven to 150C/300F/Gas2.

Drop teaspoons of the mixture onto a buttered baking tray. Bake for about half an hour till dry and set. Cut into squares or fingers.

Ingredients

- 1 cup rolled oats
- 1 cup plain flour
- ½ cup shredded coconut
- ½ cup granulated sugar
- ½ teaspoon bicarbonate of soda
- 2 tablespoons boiling water
- ½ cup butter (4 oz)
- 1 tablespoon golden syrup

Almond snaps

Very light, very crisp little Portuguese almond cookies to squirrel away in the biscuit tin for visiting grandchildren or coffee mornings. Good with ice cream.

Makes about 2 dozen

SLIVER THE ALMONDS into fine strips. Beat the butter with the sugar till light and white, fold in the flour and then stir in the shredded almonds.

Butter a baking tray and dust it with flour. Preheat the oven to 170C/325F/Gas3.

Drop little balls of the almond paste onto the prepared baking tray, leaving plenty of room for spreading. Flatten the tops with a wet teaspoon. Bake for 12–15 minutes till lacy and crisp. Transfer to a baking rack to cool.

Ingredients
- 4 oz blanched almonds
- 4 oz softened butter
- 4 oz caster sugar
- 2 oz plain flour

Chapter 10
Pickles, Jams & Preserves

Britain, said Signor Francesco Caracciolo, after touring our islands in a coach-and-four in the days when foreigners were known to be hell and abroad began at Calais, is a nation of sixty religions and only one sauce. Which statement, his hosts might well have retorted, was no more than a freedom-loving people reared on honest home cooking might expect of those accustomed to frills and frippery designed to disguise rather than enhance what nature provides.

As islanders, our culinary habits traditionally depended on ensuring that a fertile soil watered by ample rainfall, warmed by sufficient sunshine but limited by a short growing season, yielded enough in summer to fill store cupboards through the winter. Jams, pickles and preserves satisfied the need for variety in the days when fresh food was hard to come by through the cold months, when the fields were bare. Later in our culinary history, colonial involvements (to put it daintily) gave us a taste for foreign spicings, which is why and how we acquired our addiction to fiery chutneys and fruit sauces spiked with chilli.

We may no longer need to add variety to the diet – all things being available at all times at a price most of us can afford – but we still stock the store cupboard, just as granny used to do. And the results, no question, are well worth a little time and trouble.

Tomato catsup

Use field-ripened tomatoes, sweet and juicy, towards the end of the season. The misshapen or undersized ones are just what's needed. You can, if you wish, make it with unripened green tomatoes: if so, double the sugar.

Makes about 2 pints

Ingredients

- 8 lbs tomatoes
- ½ pint white malt vinegar
- 4 oz sugar
- 1 teaspoon salt
- ½ teaspoon white peppercorns
- 8 cloves
- 1 short stick cinnamon
- 1 small piece mace or 1 teaspoon freshly grated nutmeg
- 2–3 bay leaves

WASH AND ROUGHLY chop the tomatoes. Put all the ingredients into a large saucepan and leave them to infuse for half an hour. Bring the pan to the boil, turn down to a gentle simmer and leave to cook gently over a low heat for at least an hour. It shouldn't need much attention as the tomatoes produce plenty of liquid at this stage, and there is little likelihood of the mixture sticking.

Push the tomato mixture through a fine-meshed wire sieve, leaving skin, pips and spice debris behind. Return the purée to the saucepan – at this stage it will probably be far too liquid. Bring back to the boil and simmer vigorously, stirring regularly, until the sauce is as thick as you like it – it will take 30–40 minutes to reduce satisfactorily. Taste and adjust seasoning.

Bottle, cork tightly and keep in a cool place.

Worcestershire sauce

The second Baron Sandys of Worcestershire, on his return from a tour of duty in the Raj, passed on the recipe for his favourite sauce to Mr Lea of Lea & Perrins. P Morton Shand, culinary genius and great-grandfather of the future Queen Camilla, offered the recipe in his cookbook in 1927. As befits a relative of royalty, he includes sound advice to the servants: 'A great chef is witty as well as cultured in the choice of his sauces and impertinent of their use at the expense of dullard or unworthy dinners.' A little goes a long way.

Makes a pint, stores well

HAVE READY A sterilised pint bottle with a sealable top – put the bottle and its top through the dishwasher, or scald in a bowl with boiling water.

Put all the ingredients in a saucepan, bring to the boil, stir vigorously and bubble up for 15 minutes. Remove from the heat and leave to infuse overnight. Strain, bottle and seal. Ready in a week – or today, if you're in a hurry. Lay down a few bottles for later. It lasts pretty much indefinitely, improving all the time. Essential in a prairie oyster or the morning-after Bloody Mary. Use it to devil things – leftovers from the Sunday roast, cottage pie, hard-boiled eggs in curried white sauce with squishy raisins – remember those? Yum.

Ingredients

- 1 pint brown malt vinegar
- 8 oz black treacle
- 1 garlic clove
- ½ teaspoon crushed or powdered cloves
- A piece dried ginger about the size of a walnut, well crushed
- 1 dried chilli, crushed
- 1 teaspoon salt

Sauce Camelyne

A spicy sweet-sharp store cupboard sauce which served much the same function as ketchup, says Peter Brears, esteemed medievalist and author of *Cooking and Dining in Medieval England* (Prospect, 2008) – and no doubt much appreciated with barbecued bittern and spit-roast peacock. There's only so far you can take authenticity. We must content ourselves with pork pie or cold chicken or the last of the Sunday joint, all of which will benefit from a dash of medieval splendour.

Makes about a pint

SOAK THE TOAST in the vinegar and wine until soft, then rub through a sieve three times. Stir in the sugar and spices, bottle up and seal tightly. Store in the fridge (not very medieval, I know – but they didn't have central heating).

For a green sauce, omit the spices and add 2 oz mixed fresh herbs – parsley, mint, sorrel, chives – ground to a paste.

Ingredients

- 8 oz white bread, sliced and toasted golden brown
- ¼ pint white wine vinegar
- ¼ pint white wine
- 4 teaspoons sugar
- Pinch of saffron
- ¼ teaspoon ground cinnamon
- ¼ teaspoon ground ginger
- ¼ teaspoon ground cloves

Honey-pickled courgettes

A useful recipe for anyone with a glut of courgettes – once they start they never seem to stop – from *The Perfect Pickle Book* by David Mabey and David Collison, first published in the 1980s and reprinted by Grub Street in 2007.

Makes about 1 lb

SPRINKLE THE COURGETTE slices with a little salt in a colander and leave for an hour to drain. Mix the turmeric, ½ teaspoon salt, mustard seeds, honey and vinegar in a small pan, bring to the boil and simmer for 3 minutes. Remove and leave to cool.

Rinse the salt off the courgettes, drain and pat dry. Layer with the onion rings into warm sterilised jars. Pour in enough spiced vinegar to cover everything completely. Seal and store for 2–3 days before eating. Keeps for weeks in the fridge.

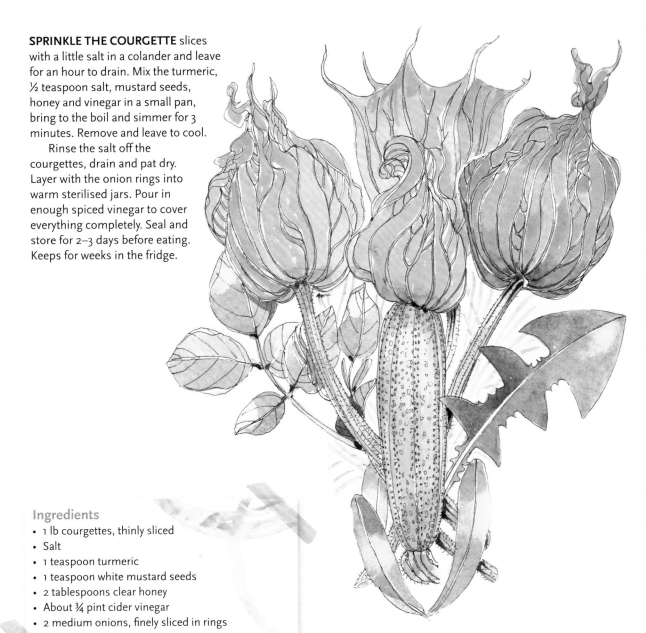

Ingredients
- 1 lb courgettes, thinly sliced
- Salt
- 1 teaspoon turmeric
- 1 teaspoon white mustard seeds
- 2 tablespoons clear honey
- About ¾ pint cider vinegar
- 2 medium onions, finely sliced in rings

Mushroom ketchup

Ketchup, say those who know such things, is a descendant of the Oriental fermented fish sauces which are, as I'm sure you know, pretty much the same thing as the Roman *garum*. Mushroom ketchup, on the other hand, is a descendant of the medieval housewife's mushroom pickle, a preparation which included neither sugar nor vinegar. Good with fishcakes or a breakfast fry-up, and great in gravies.

Makes about 1 ½ pints

Ingredients
- 4 lbs flat black mushrooms
- 4 oz salt
- 1 teaspoon black peppercorns
- 1 teaspoon crushed mace
- 1 teaspoon grated nutmeg
- 1 pint malt vinegar
- ¼ pint brandy

HAVE READY SOME sterilised bottles. Wipe the mushrooms and layer them in the bowl, scattering salt between each layer. Weight with a clean plate and leave overnight to make juice.

The next day, crush the spices and bring them to the boil with the vinegar. Pour the vinegar over the mushrooms, stir, and tip everything into a roomy saucepan. Bring all to the boil and bubble roundly for 15 minutes. Stir in the brandy and remove from the heat.

You now have a choice – thick or thin? Thick is my own favourite, thin has a longer shelf life. Either strain off the liquid and pour it directly, still hot, into the sterilised bottles and seal tightly. Or allow it to cool, dump the contents of the pan into the liquidiser and process to a thick purée. Return the mixture to the pan and bring back to the boil, then bottle as above. Store in a cool, dark place. Ready in a week.

Sir James Ranald Martin's rhubarb chutney

Sir James was a conscientious Scot, a friend of Florence Nightingale (not an easy row to hoe, by all accounts), who took commission with the East India Company and collected recipes from the courts of the rajahs through the early 1800s. More of the same in *The Road to Vindaloo* by David Burnett and Helen Saberi (Prospect, 2008).

Makes about 4 lbs

WASH, STRIP AND cut up the rhubarb very finely. Skin the lemons, cut the pulp finely, removing the pips. Cut and crush the garlic very fine. Bruise the ginger. Put the whole of your ingredients into the pan and boil till the mixture becomes very thick. Pick out the ginger, and then cover the mixture in a jar. Keep one month before using.

Ingredients
- 2 lbs rhubarb
- 8 oz sultanas
- 1 lb sugar
- 2 lemons
- 1 oz garlic
- 1 oz ginger
- 1 pint vinegar

Sir James was a conscientious Scot, who took commission with the East India Company and collected recipes from the courts of the rajahs through the early 1800s

English salad cream

Much nicer than the vinegary stuff you get in a bottle, this smooth, creamy pourable sauce is thickened over hot water in much the same way as a custard. It seems to have fallen out of favour around the time we northerners discovered olive oil and the joys of bottled mayonnaise.

Makes about a pint

PUT ALL THE ingredients in the liquidiser and process thoroughly, or whisk together by hand.

Transfer to a bowl set over simmering water as if for a custard, and whisk over the heat for as long as it takes for the mixture to coat the back of a wooden spoon (this is a pouring sauce, don't expect it to thicken like a mayonnaise). Taste, adjust the seasoning, and carry on whisking for another few minutes to make sure the raw flour is cooked. Transfer to sterilised bottles and cork down. Keep in a cool place. Ready immediately – and stays good, unopened, for months.

Ingredients
- 1 egg plus 2 yolks
- ¼ pint thick cream
- ½ pint milk
- 4–6 tablespoons cider or malt vinegar
- 1 heaped tablespoon plain flour
- ½ teaspoon mustard powder
- 1 teaspoon salt
- ½ teaspoon freshly milled white pepper

Home-made Nutella

This is a pretty good copy of the preparation known to my New York granddaughters as 'chocolate heaven'. The real thing is pretty well unobtainable in the States and I'm tired of lugging the stuff around in my transatlantic luggage, not to mention needing to explain myself to customs when the sniffer dogs get wind.

Makes about 1 lb

PUT THE SUGAR and cocoa in a saucepan and stir until blended. Gradually stir in the milk. Bring to the boil over a gentle heat, stirring constantly, then lower the heat and simmer for 2 minutes. Remove from the heat and leave to cool for at least 5 minutes. Add the vanilla essence, peanut butter and ground hazelnuts, stirring till perfectly amalgamated. Leave to cool, and pot up in a jar.

Ingredients

- 5 oz sugar
- 2 oz unsweetened cocoa powder
- Scant ½ pint milk
- 1 teaspoon vanilla essence
- 2 tablespoons smooth peanut butter
- 1 heaped tablespoon ground hazelnuts

> *This is a pretty good copy of the preparation known to my New York granddaughters as 'chocolate heaven'. The real thing is pretty well unobtainable in the States and I'm tired of lugging the stuff around in my transatlantic luggage*

Redcurrant and raspberry confiture

French confitures are closer to a compote than a jam, delivering a short shelf life but a fabulous flavour. The balance of fruits is important: redcurrants are high in pectin, the substance which allows the juice to jellify, while raspberries have very little.

Makes about 5 lbs

CRUSH THE RASPBERRIES with the currants – use the liquidiser – and then crush through a sieve to extract all the juice.

Weigh the juice, and for each lb of juice allow 1 ½ lbs sugar. Stir the sugar into the juice while cooking on a gentle heat until the crystals have completely dissolved, then pour the juice into small sterilised jars. Lid or cover tightly while still hot. Put the jars out in the sunshine for 8 hours in the middle of the day for 2 days running. If sunshine is not available, a very low oven would do. Store in a cool place. If you fail to achieve a set (modern soft fruit cultivation and artificial ripening processes can sometimes produce weird results), bottle it up and use as a coulis – delicious warmed and poured over vanilla ice cream.

Ingredients
- 2 lbs raspberries
- 4 lbs redcurrants
- 3–4 lbs granulated sugar

Strawberry preserve

While British jam traditions tend to call for rather a lot of sugar and prolonged boiling – precautions taken against the hazards of a damp climate – Continental preserves aim to conserve the natural colour and taste of the fruit. The price is a short shelf life, so best stored in the fridge. If you use preserving sugar – that is, sugar fortified with pectin – you'll achieve a firmer set and longer shelf life but lose something of the purity of flavour.

Makes about 6 lbs

RINSE AND HULL the strawberries.

Put the sugar and ¼ pint water in a heavy preserving pan and bring it slowly to the boil, stirring to dissolve the sugar crystals. Skim and bubble up until a little of it dropped in cold water forms a soft ball – 238F/114C on the sugar thermometer.

Add the strawberries and put the pan on the side of the stove to draw the juice. Leave for 10 minutes. Remove the berries to a bowl with a draining spoon. Bring the syrup back to the boil until it reaches the soft-ball stage again. Leave to cool for 10 minutes. Bring to the boil for a third time. When it reaches soft-ball stage, add the strawberries and boil for 5–10 minutes, until the juice falls in thick clinging drops from the spoon.

Leave to cool overnight. Pot up in small sterilised jars, top with a round of greaseproof paper dipped in brandy. Seal tightly and store in the fridge. Gorgeous as a dessert with *fromage frais*, or spooned over vanilla ice cream, or just as it comes with scones and clotted cream for tea.

Ingredients
- 4 lbs firm ripe strawberries
- 2 lbs granulated or preserving sugar

Peach marmalade

The American way with a popular Mediterranean preserve – *mermelada* being the name given to all things jammy in places where orange marmalade is something weird demanded by tourists. The recipe was brought to my attention by the late scholar cook M F K Fisher, a name to conjure with, Stateside. And very good it is too.

Makes about 3 lbs

SCALD AND PEEL the peaches, cut them in half and remove the stones. Crack 5 of the stones, extract the kernels and stew them in a little water in a small pan for 5 minutes until tender; then skin and chop.

Put the peaches and kernels in a large saucepan and bring slowly to boiling point, mashing the peaches with a potato masher as they heat. By time the mixture boils, the peaches should be really mushy. Stir in the sugar and the lemon juice and cook rapidly for 10 minutes, stirring all the time –

it may look juicy enough, but it can easily stick and burn. Turn down the heat and cook slowly for about another 5 minutes. It should be ready by now, but maybe you'd better put a test spoonful on a cold saucer in the refrigerator just to be sure of the set.

Pour the jam into clean sterilised jars and seal it down. Ready immediately. Not a good keeper, though there'll probably be no need to put longevity to the test. If you've made it in quantity, store in the freezer.

Ingredients
- 2 lbs peaches (about 8 peaches)
- 1 lb granulated sugar
- Juice of 2 lemons

Cheat's Pimm's

This is neither a pickle nor a preserve but might go some way to pickling and preserving you! This version is Jane MacQuitty's recipe for what is basically a diluted gin sling, as consumed by old India-hands on the verandah at sundown in Poona. The combination, it's said, was invented by James Pimm in 1823. Ms MacQuitty's version tastes just as good and is a lot better value than the ready-mix. Bottoms up.

FOR EVERY MEASURE of good 40 per cent-plus gin, add a measure of red vermouth – French or Italian – plus half a measure of orange curaçao. Give the mixture a chance to mingle and marry for several hours and add a slice each per person of lemon, orange, strawberry and cucumber. A sprig of mint and borage adds pleasing herby overtones. Top up with ice-cold fizzy lemonade or ginger beer. One part Cheat's Pimm's to four parts fizz is the happiest ratio.

> *This is a recipe for what is basically a diluted gin sling, as consumed by old India-hands on the verandah at sundown in Poona*

Conversion tables

A guide to converting imperial measures to metric or cup measures

USING CUP AND SPOON MEASURES

*All cup and spoon measures should be level
(unless otherwise stated)*

¼ teaspoon	1.25 ml
½ teaspoon	2.5 ml
1 teaspoon	5 ml
1 tablespoon	15 ml

WEIGHTS

Imperial	Metric	Imperial	Metric
¼ lb	100 g	1 lb 2 oz	500 g
6 oz	175 g	1 ¼ lb	575 g
½ lb	225 g	1 ½ lb	675 g
12 oz	350 g	1 ¾ lb	800 g
1 lb	450 g	2 ¼ lb	1 kg

OVEN TEMPERATURES

°C	°F	Gas
110	225	¼
120	250	½
140	275	1
150	300	2
160	325	3
180	350	4
190	375	5
200	400	6
220	425	7
230	450	8
250	475	9

LIQUID MEASURES

Imperial	Metric	Cup
2 fl oz	60 ml	¼ cup
8 fl oz	250 ml	1 cup
½ pint	300 ml	1 ¼ cups
12 fl oz	350 ml	1 ½ cups
14 fl oz	400 ml	1 ¾ cups
16 fl oz	475 ml	2 cups
1 pint	600 ml	2 ½ cups
1 ¼ pints	750 ml	3 cups
1 ¾ pints	1 litre	4 cups

BASIC INGREDIENTS

Cup and weight equivalents

Breadcrumbs, dry	2 ½ oz / 65 g = 1 cup
Breadcrumbs, fresh	2 oz / 50 g = 1 cup
Butter	8 oz / 225 g = 1 cup 8 tablespoons / 100 g = 1 stick
Cheese, grated cheddar	4 oz / 100 g = 1 cup
Icing sugar	4 oz / 100 g = 1 cup
Cornflour	8 oz / 225 g = 1 cup
Cream cheese, ricotta	8 oz / 225 g = 1 cup
Flour	4 oz / 100 g = 1 cup
Honey	8 oz / 225 g = 1 cup
Parmesan cheese, grated	3 oz / 75 g = 1 cup
Peas, frozen	4 oz / 100 g = 1 cup
Polenta	5 oz / 150 g = 1 cup
Rice, long-grain types	200 g / 7 oz = 1 cup
Sugar, granulated or caster	8 oz / 225 g = 1 cup (generous) 7 oz / 200 g = 1 cup (scant)

Index

Acknowledgement
'Lamb Korma' from *Curry, a biography* by Lizzie
Collingham, published by Chatto & Windus.
Reprinted by permission of The Random House Group Ltd.